MARTIN SHAW

MARTIN SHAW

THE BIOGRAPHY

STAFFORD HILDRED
AND TIM EWBANK

JOHN BLAKE

Published by John Blake Publishing Ltd,
3 Bramber Court, 2 Bramber Road,
London W14 9PB, England

www.blake.co.uk

First published in hardback in 2006

ISBN 1 84454 295 5

British Library Cataloguing-in-Publication Data:

A catalogue record for this book is available from the British Library.

Design by www.envydesign.co.uk

Printed in Great Britain by Creative Print and Design, Wales

1 3 5 7 9 10 8 6 4 2

Papers used by John Blake Publishing are natural, recyclable products made from wood
grown in sustainable forests. The manufacturing processes conform to the environmental
regulations of the country of origin.

Every attempt has been made to contact the relevant copyright-holders, but some were
unobtainable. We would be grateful if the appropriate people could contact us.

Tim Ewbank
To my mother Joy for her wonderful love, support
and encouragement.

Stafford Hildred
To my wife Janet and daughters Claire and Rebecca.

For their co-operation and help; John and Tyna Airey,
Jay Bowers, John and Pippa Burmester, Brian Clemens,
Lewis Collins, Peter Coppock, Roger and Dr Jutta Davis,
Maggie Forwood, Rod and Joy Gilchrist, Kathryn Holcombe,
Hazel Hyslop, Clive Jackson, Gordon Jackson, Selina Julien,
Paula Jones, Barry Kernon, Hilary Kingsley, Alan Kingston,
Simon Kinnersley, Frank and Hazel Langan, Zoe MacIntyre,
Paul McNichol, Moira Marr, Fraser Massey, Kit Miller,
Keith Richmond, Alasdair Riley, Vanda Rumney, Brian Tesler.
And special thanks to Emma and Oliver Ewbank.

ACKNOWLEDGEMENTS

The authors would like to acknowledge the following as important sources of information; *Daily Express*, *Daily Mail*, *Mirror*, *Radio Times*, *TV Times*, *Sun*, *News of the World*, *The Times*, *Evening Standard*, *Woman's Own*, *Primetime* magazine, BBC Radio 1, BBC Radio 2, BBC Radio 4.

Special thanks must go to Channel 4's *Within These Walls* programme about *The Professionals* which provided invaluable information and observations from the show's actors and creator Brian Clemens.

Stafford and Tim would also like to thank Dave Matthews who expertly runs *The Professionals* website which provides fascinating and detailed information about the TV show.

We would also like to thank the many actors, writers, producers, directors and assorted friends and colleagues who were happy to share their memories of Martin Shaw, but who preferred to remain anonymous. Thanks to Garth Pearce and Ian Woodward.

The authors would also especially like to thank Clive Hebard for his enthusiastic input, and all at Blake Publishing.

CONTENTS

WHEELS OF FORTUNE

'He hit me hard and I went sailing through the air and hit
the road face first'
Martin Shaw on the motorbike accident
that could have cost him his life

It is 25 years since Martin Shaw's love of speed almost cost him his life in 1981, but he can remember it as if it were yesterday. In a hurry as usual, Martin was pushing his beloved BMW R100RS motorbike as fast as he dared while overtaking two lines of frustrated backed-up traffic on London's North Circular Road. He was concentrating hard on staying just inside the white line and constantly checking to make sure there was no right turn ahead and nowhere for any of the trapped cars and lorries to go. Then suddenly, his motorcycle was sideswiped by a car that pulled out in front of him very fast.

'I can only think that because of the traffic jam he'd got

irritated and decided to do a U-turn,' said Martin. 'And that's something you can't predict. He hit me hard and I went sailing through the air and hit the road face first. The next thing I saw was an artic coming towards me on the other side of the road!'

Instinctively, he carried on rolling, very fast across the road and he even managed to bump up the kerb on the other side. It all happened much too fast for him to realise exactly what was happening and afterwards he decided he must have been knocked out as soon as he hit the road, although he did recall a painful glimpse of his bike somersaulting end over end down the carriageway.

At the time, *The Professionals* was the hottest show on television, so seeing Martin Shaw performing death-defying stunts was nothing out of the ordinary. But this time as he gingerly began to recover there was no director to shout 'Cut!'. After he had finally stopped rolling, Martin finished on the edge of the road. He was semi-conscious and at first unable to move. His visor was shattered but miraculously he escaped without any real injury. As the feeling gradually came back into his body he was able to think that he must not move because he might have broken bones or internal injuries. People rushed to his side wondering if they had just witnessed yet another motorcycling fatality.

'There were people talking to me, but because the front of the helmet and visor was smashed, they didn't know if I was dead or not,' said Martin. 'Obviously I wasn't dead and I wasn't even badly hurt. I found that everything moved and I hadn't broken a thing. I had been really, really lucky.'

The bike was pretty badly damaged but the driver who

pulled out and caused the crash admitted his guilt, and the driver of the artic. and two other motorists offered to explain what had happened. Martin was very grateful: 'So many people these days don't want the hassle and don't want to get involved.'

Such a terrifying accident might have pushed some motorbike enthusiasts to the comparative safety of four wheels but not Shaw. A few months later he took delivery of an electrifyingly swift F1-spec Honda.

CHILDHOOD

'I enjoyed the experience so much I wouldn't leave the stage'
Martin Shaw on his first stage appearance at the age of 3

The Birmingham suburb of Erdington was briefly mentioned in the Domesday Book under its earlier name of Hardintone, but it never seemed to really come into its own until the engineering industry arrived in the city in the nineteenth century. Then the giant Fort Dunlop building came to dominate the local skyline and became Britain's largest poster site, just as the production of the motor car drove the local economy.

Famous residents are distinctly thin on the ground, according to the average Yentonian (as Erdington residents are known), though the controversial newspaper columnist Richard Littlejohn once lived there. Erdington does have its own abbey, which is an outstanding example of Gothic Revival architecture. Also, from 1968 to 1971, Erdington was home to the famous rock music venue, Mothers, where Traffic appropriately made their world debut and bands like The Who, Black Sabbath and Deep Purple performed. As the late John Peel once said: 'People are amazed to hear that for a few years the best club in Britain was in Erdington!' And, most noticeably, the district is now bordered by the astonishing road junction that was christened the Gravelly Hill Multi-Level Interchange – better known as Spaghetti Junction.

However, so far as we, the authors, could detect there is as yet no shiny blue plaque to mark the site of the house on Lovesey Street, Erdington where Martin Shaw lived with his family for the first 11 years of his life after first coming into the world on 21 January 1945. It was a grim time, with the last battles of World War II still being fought out. Birmingham was a city of shortages and damaged buildings; young Martin arrived in a world desperately weary of conflict, but fortunately for him he came into a warm and loving family. His father Frank was a sales engineer in the heating business and his mother Jo was a champion ballroom dancer who was vivacious and beautiful, and always looked very young for her age. More than once in the years to come, much to her delight, she was mistaken for Martin's sister.

He got the acting bug very early. 'My parents were both artistically inclined and they were very keen on amateur dramatics. When I was 3 they took part in a revue and I made my first stage appearance in it. I wore a straw boater and spectacles with a pipe in my mouth and held a carrier bag. I was told to walk across the stage, look at the audience, wait until they laughed and then drop the pipe out of my mouth into the carrier bag. I didn't understand anything about it, of course, but it brought the house down. I enjoyed the experience so much I wouldn't leave the stage. I loved the applause but I hadn't learned anything about entrances and exits and finally I had to be lifted bodily over the footlights by my father.' A little later the whole family got involved in a street party and Frank played Al Jolson, Martin's grandmother Agnes was Al's Mammy and Martin himself took off Arthur English's popular spiv act, offering nylons for sale to all the girls. All three of them won prizes.

Money was frequently short in those post-war years but Martin's parents somehow always managed to provide a holiday for the family. When Martin was 4½ for instance, they spent a blissful week in a caravan at Golden Sands at Rhyl.

The famous Spitfire factory was just down the road in Castle Bromwich and even as a very young boy Martin was always totally fascinated by aircraft. It was a passion he must have inherited from his father that became one of the many strong bonds between the two of them. Father and son spent hours locked together by their love of aeroplanes. 'I've been a real aircraft nut as for long as I can remember,' said Martin. 'Anything to do with aircraft that I could read, or buy, or make... I would. My dad loved aeroplanes as well so I'm sure it came from him. We used to make Airfix models and go to airshows together.' But Frank helped encourage his son's interest in all sorts of subjects, as Martin once said: '...From astrology to zoology. And it is his knowledge and interest and endlessly enquiring mind that has helped me throughout my life.'

There was never too much money about in those heavily

rationed and restricted post-war days and Martin's parents had to work hard to provide for the family. But they shared a belief that entertainment and education were important aspects of life and they were both determined to stimulate and inspire their young son. Martin's younger brother Jeremy, who was forever known as Jem, came along when Martin was 7.

Girls entered Shaw's life in a big way somewhat later on but, he recalled, not too seriously: 'My first love was a girl at primary school. Her name was Marie. She was very tall for a 10-year-old, with very blonde hair and very blue eyes. I was totally smitten. There were smiles and blushes but it never went any further.'

On another occasion he spotted a pretty girl who was playing on the top of an old baker's van. Young Martin climbed up to join her to try to chat her up and the girl's twin brother arrived and threatened him: 'If you don't come down from there I'll knock you off!' With the sort of fearless disregard for his own safety that has landed him in trouble more than once in his life, Martin refused to back down. 'I said, "You and whose army?" And he climbed up and knocked me off! Just like that. It's funny how you meet your friends, because he became one of my best mates and I used to see him every time I went home.'

'We lived in Erdington until I was 11,' Martin said. 'My parents and myself – and later my brother – shared a World War I council house with my maternal grandparents. My grandmother was like a second mother to me. She had an enormous influence on me. She was a wonderfully imposing figure. She didn't have bosoms, instead she had a kind of bolster like a sort of mobile hanging shelf. It was an Edwardian shape

8

that you don't really seem to see these days. The house had a range with an open fire and we still had gas mantles. My grandfather's bedroom was lit by a gas mantle, which he kept going all night. God knows what that did to his breathing! My mother's passion was ballroom dancing and she used to win competitions in Warwickshire and Birmingham. She absolutely adored it and she could do all the flowing head turns and the incredibly intricate steps.'

There was a real warmth and openness about family life and Martin recalls there were always challenging arguments going on about the issues of the day and even a young voice was able to find an audience. 'Of course I took my parents and grandparents completely for granted,' said Martin. 'Who doesn't? But later I knew how fortunate I had been with my upbringing. Times probably were pretty hard for them when I was little but I must have been very well protected from that. Laughter and happy voices are my main memories of growing up and I know now that makes me a very lucky guy.'

A happy upbringing does not necessarily mean a dull one. Martin recalls handling guns from being a very small boy. His grandfather was a gunsmith in Birmingham. 'My grandfather used to work in a shed at the bottom of the garden,' he said. 'He would never allow anyone in while he was working but I used to peep through a hole and watch. It was like an Aladdin's cave in there to me. There was my grandfather tapping away with a little copper hammer at the stock of a sporting gun, hammering in bits of silver chasing. It was a rare occasion indeed for me to be allowed to hold one of these works of art, because that is what they were.'

Then, when Martin was leaving primary school, his parents managed to buy a house in Streetly, Sutton Coldfield, which was a huge step. It was the fulfilment of a lifelong dream for Martin's father Frank. He had always wanted a place of his own, preferably further out of the busy city and within reach of some countryside. 'Nowadays people's impossible dream seems to be to win the Lottery,' says Martin. 'Ours was to simply buy a house and a car. It seemed out of reach for a long time so to have achieved both aims felt amazing.'

When Martin was growing up as a teenager, Sutton Coldfield was on the edge of farmland. But although he had put a little distance between himself and Birmingham he retained a strong Brummie accent and a great affection for his birthplace. For many years afterwards his parents remained living in the same small semi-detached house which meant so much to them. It was a real family home. 'It might not have been very big at all, but it felt like a mansion,' he recalls fondly.

In his early teens, Martin joined the local Sea Scouts. He was a keen member for a while, until playing make-believe sailors landed him in trouble, thanks to his acute sense of humour. Martin's natural sense of fun would bubble over into giggles when they were required to 'pipe' people aboard ship, which was just the top half of an old boat planted on the grass in a local park. He was thrown out for not playing the game!

At secondary school he struggled to make any sort of mark for quite a while. He loved playing football and quickly made friends, but in the classroom he spent most of his days dreaming about aircraft or waiting impatiently for the lesson to be over. By his own account he was inclined to be untidy, absent-minded, clumsy, fragile, over-sensitive and a popular target for bullying.

'I was a bit of a whimperer, I suppose,' says Martin, with his own brand of brutal honesty. 'But I do remember a few useful lessons from my childhood. Dad used to say, "Bullies are always scared. If you stand up to them, they'll back down." But for a long time I was always too scared to put that theory to the test. There was one particular bully at our school and he was being such a nightmare that it got to the point where I thought, "I've got nothing to lose if I end up having his fist halfway down my throat." It couldn't be any worse than I was already going through. He kept on and on, and one of the techniques to make the weakly kids miserable was to say, "I'm going to get you tonight outside school." You had the whole day to suffer. So one day, as he was pushing me around, he said, "I'm going to be waiting outside school and I'll get you." I thought, "This is insane. I'm going to get hit anyway so let him just do it and get it over with." So I planted my feet apart and put my fists up and said, "Don't wait for tonight, do it now." The look on his face was extraordinary. I said, "Come on, I'm ready." I looked him right in the eyes and I saw that he was frightened. Also there were a lot of other kids around saying, "Go on then, do it." He started to back away and said, "No." That changed my attitude a bit. I was never bullied again. And I knew then that you don't have to be timid.'

Martin was always very keen to get behind the wheel of a car and learn to drive. 'My dad used to let me drive whenever we were off public roads so I knew the basics from about the age of 12 onwards,' he said. 'When I had lessons to take my test, years later, I found I only needed six and passed first time, but I was very nervous. At one point the examiner asked me what the speed limit was. I said, "30" and he said, "Yes, that means you can actually reach that speed." I had been driving at about 18 mph.'

Martin's mental strength is one of his most remarkable facets and perhaps the root of that extraordinary stillness and self-confidence goes back to his formative years. 'I had unusual parents in that they were spiritually agnostic,' he says. 'They were also extremely open-minded. If a Jehovah's Witness came to the door he would not be turned away. The man's opinions might not get across but he would always be invited to state his case. I grew up in awe of my father's quest for truth. We were always having intense discussions of all faiths; he would never accept any kind of dogma. The house was always filled with brilliant, but sometimes heated discussions. Ministers and vicars loved him but there was a time when they would shake their heads and, "Oh, but Frank, you really must conform to the scriptures you know." ... My father followed no religion at all but he believed in God. He was a Christian in the broadest sense, that he always espoused the Christian ideals of love and kindness. Where he would sometimes become unpopular is that he would say a flower had as much soul as you or I.' But the heated discussions were simply an integral part of family life to Shaw and nothing was out of bounds.

Sometimes the family even took part in a kind of séance. Martin explained: 'We would put our fingers on the glass and it would go shooting round the table. The greatest thing is doing it with your own family because you know no one is cheating. You put letters of the alphabet round the table and the touch on the glass is so light.'

He found these experiences deeply life-enhancing and he tried to always keep an open mind, particularly when others are jumping to more obvious conclusions. 'What I have learned,' he said, 'is that mind is not limited to the head or to people who are alive. At the moment it is not possible to see or photograph a thought. A hundred years ago we had not learned how to use electricity which has always been there.'

One experience of moving the glass around the letters left a deep impression on him. 'My grandfather was a very dry person,' he recalled. 'He would not say much for a whole afternoon and then only a few words. A few years after his death we had a whole conversation lasting over an hour – so much his character, even the energy in which he talked. At one point he said, "Suck the broth." My father, Jem and myself thought, "What's this?" But my mother said it was something he said if you fell over or something. Just an expression, "Oh, never mind, suck the broth."'

Not that all conversations were mystical, highbrow or pretentious in the Shaw household by any means. Martin also recalls that for long periods he nursed rather more mundane fantasies about the future involving him working as a vet and later as a train driver. He also developed an early interest in music. Elvis Presley was one of his early heroes. At one point he was quite fanatical in his enthusiasm at and was determined to copy the highly distinctive Presley hairstyle. 'I used to envy Elvis because he could grease his hair back,' says Martin. 'But

I've got a double crown and my hair grows in opposite directions. I used to dip my comb in Brylcreem and run it through my hair trying to make it look like Elvis's and it never seemed to look right. My mother even permed it for me when I was 14 and desperate.'

There is an intense and stubborn side to his character that can upset people. 'I suppose it started at school,' he said. 'I refused to conform and believe that exams were an important part of evaluating someone's intelligence. It may sound big-headed but I thought I was too bright to pass exams. I was even beaten because I wouldn't learn everything parrot fashion.'

In many lessons Martin floundered and he had no real clue what sort of a career he might choose. 'I don't think acting was ever thought about,' he said. 'The only thing I was any good at was English Language and I certainly enjoyed poetry. Everything else I was equally bad at and when the careers officer came along the only thing they could come up with was librarian and I thought, "Oh God!" The prospect of living your life in hushed tones clearly did not appeal.

The most significant moment of Shaw's schooldays was the first time his class were asked to read Shakespeare. 'For the very first time I got to feel like other people felt in maths classes,' he smiled many years later. Even then he admitted that the mention of 'double maths' was enough to send a shiver down his spine. 'In maths it seemed as if everyone knew what was going on while I hadn't got a clue. Suddenly the situation was reversed. Nobody knew what the play was about except me. And I couldn't understand why nobody understood it; it was just so clear to me. The first thing we read out loud was *Julius*

Caesar and I found that in playing Brutus and Cassius – the teacher would change the parts around – I really got into it and could understand what was going on. The next play we read was *Macbeth* and it was on the GCE syllabus that year and they did it as a school play, and I played Macduff and I realised acting was something I could do.'

An inspirational drama teacher called Tom Knowles suggested an alternative to the proposed career as a librarian by getting Martin into the school drama club. His first reaction was not promising. '"No! That's cissy," I thought,' says Martin. But the dedicated Mr Knowles was a fierce defender of drama and would always leap to the attack if anyone wrote off his subject as a 'pansy' option (in the phrase of the day). 'But then it occurred to me that here was a chance to be good at something, instead of being the person who was always spoken of in terms of "Guess who came bottom again?"'

Drama was the only thing that fired him at school. 'Tom Knowles was an incredible teacher who would get us into the school hall, play some Bach and tell us to dance. We would say, "Don't be so stupid." He'd clip someone round the ear and we would start to dance. It was amazing, all these rough, football-playing Birmingham kids flitting round in a free-expression ballet. But it gave me my first interest in acting.'

He was delighted that at last he had found something he was good at. In 1961, aged 16, as he left school he was offered a scholarship to drama school but his parents felt that he was too young. Instead he went to work in the sales office of a company that manufactured a metal-finishing machine called the Lachromatic Vibrator. Martin was not impressed by the company's standard sales letter and, with the sublime confidence of youth, he wrote a new one of his own! It could of course have landed him the sack but in fact his boss was quick to note the improvement and immediately promoted him to a more senior position in the Direct Sales department, complete with his own secretary, no less. But by then he was beginning to realise that acting was more than just something he was good at; it was becoming something he simply had to do. And his sales success had brought out a side of him that he did not like. 'I was arrogant,' he admits. 'I pushed people about so much I couldn't keep a secretary for more than a few weeks.' Martin's growing self-awareness told him that he was approaching a major turning point in his life.

But he did not put quite all of his energies into the day job. The influential Tom Knowles had by then formed a semi-professional drama group called The Pied Piper Players and Martin was swiftly recruited. The Pied Pipers were a *commedia dell'arte* group who got together twice a week to decide what show to put on, rehearse and practise on their instruments for the musical side of the show. Then they went out and put on a show every Sunday. They would use all sorts of venues from the streets to any one of the many Birmingham bomb sites. He explained: 'Sometimes we would hire the school hall and decide on a scenario, either using traditional stories like *The Sleeping Beauty* or making up a play of our own. We never learned our words or anything, and the spectators sometimes determined which way the action would go. They would get so carried away with it that we would occasionally have to restrain them. "Right kids," we said once, "we need six hefty

16

policemen to come and beat up the wicked man!" and the poor actor got so bruised and knocked about that we had to cut that scene.'

Martin loved it. 'Sometimes it was just brilliant when the kids would follow us until we found some open land,' he said. 'Then we would set up shop and give a performance. It really was like being a Pied Piper, a fantastic experience. The children were our sternest critics but they loved the company.' He even began to look like an actor. Sloppy-Joe sweaters, tight jeans and sandals were his usual mode of dress and he made several trips to nearby Stratford-upon-Avon to, as he put it, 'eat up the Shakespeare' – more than once with his girlfriend at the time, who was his first real love. She was quite a character and Martin said later: 'She would embarrass me when we would haunt the actors' pubs afterwards by wearing a green bowler hat. I think she must have been the first genuine eccentric I had ever met – she was quite a girl.' The strong theatrical influences combined to give him the increased momentum to want to try to make acting his career.

'I auditioned for some London drama schools and got into LAMDA [the London Academy of Music and Dramatic Art],' says Martin, 'which was more than a little lucky because in 1963 it was the best in the world – I didn't know that at the time, of course.'

It must be said that in his late teens Martin Shaw was not at all the clean-living, non-drinking, non-smoking picture of health that theatre and television audiences have come to know and love over the years. He says: 'I started drinking halves of bitter when I was 14. I always had quite a weak frame as a younger boy, but at 15 I started to fill out and when I was 18 or 19 I got really bulky, thanks partly to the beer I suppose. As soon as I got my freedom to go to places on my own I started to frequent jazz clubs and for a while I became a beatnik. I also started to drink even more heavily which is probably why I kept putting on weight.'

LAMDA

'Somehow the school discovered a sensitivity beneath my roughshod, drinking, big-headed character and they brought this out. It altered my personality completely'
Martin Shaw on his student days at the
London Academy of Music and Dramatic Art

Martin Shaw might not have realised it but he could hardly have headed for drama college in London at a more exciting time for a young man. Not for nothing had the Americans dubbed the capital Swinging London: youth held sway amid a colourful explosion of creativity in music, art, fashion, photography, movies and the theatre. They were exciting times, and it was 'Cool Britannia'. David Bailey was the photographer of the day, Jean Shrimpton and Twiggy ruled the world of modelling, Mary Quant had launched the mini-skirt, Michael Caine and Terence Stamp were the two young London actors the film world was talking about, the Rolling

Stones were pop gods and clubs like the Scotch of St. James, the Speakeasy and the Cromwellian were packed every night with peacock males dressed garishly by Carnaby Street, who were dancing the night away with dolly-bird girlfriends who felt liberated by the advent of the Pill. The feel-good factor was tangible: England had won the World Cup at Wembley, all over the world the Beatles were top of the charts and at the box office with *Yellow Submarine*, and Paul Scofield was on his way to winning an Oscar for his role as Sir Thomas More in the movie *A Man For All Seasons*.

Martin arrived in 1963, not so much in style but astride his closest companion – his aged but lovingly restored motorbike, an A7 Combo that had cost him all of £15 back home. 'It took me a whole year to get the bike into mint condition,' he said nostalgically, years later. 'I must have visited every breaker's yard in Brum.' Of course, in those days Birmingham was the motorcycle capital of the world so that must have meant a lot of breaker's yards. 'It was a beautiful bike – bloody beautiful,' he recalled.

At the London Academy of Music and Dramatic Art, he was able to mingle with other like-minded students drawn from all areas of the country. The days when rounded vowels were de rigueur for entry to top London drama schools had long gone, and a Birmingham accent would be no drawback. He could also pride himself on being a student at one of the very best drama colleges in the world. LAMDA had a proud history that dated back to 1861, making the Academy the oldest of its kind in Britain. Apart from moving to Hampton Court for a brief period during World War II when its studios were bombed, the Academy had always been based in west London and when Martin was a student its home was in Earl's Court. Among its notable Alumni are the late Richard Harris, David Suchet, Maureen Lipman, Brian Cox (a contemporary of Martin's) and Patricia Hodge, who was much later to play a somewhat upmarket girlfriend of Martin's character Ray Doyle in *The Professionals*.

Martin proved to be an exceptional pupil who frequently stood out from the others and the LAMDA course also became a passage of personal discovery. The Academy prided itself, as it does today, in neither seeking to teach skills superficially, nor to deconstruct the individual in order to rebuild a LAMDA product. Rather, the aim was to encourage and develop talents already innate in each student, all of which suited him perfectly. 'Somehow the school discovered a sensitivity beneath my roughshod, drinking, big-headed character and they brought this out,' he was able to say on looking back. 'It altered my personality completely.'

He will always be grateful to LAMDA, where he learned so much of his craft. 'It changed me from an adolescent into a man,' said Martin. 'The timing was perfect,' he later observed. 'The extremes of Method acting were starting to go away, the "scratch your arse, kick pebbles and mumble" techniques were on the way out. I just happened to hit a wonderful couple of years – I was very lucky.'

Martin's trusty motorbike faced a pretty comprehensive change as well. Years later, in a hilarious interview with a motorbike magazine, he recalled: 'I went out to Hampton Court one day with a girlfriend and it was incredibly hot weather. I was showing off and really thrashing it (the bike!). One of the nuts came loose on the carb through vibration. It dripped petrol on to the exhaust, which was already overheating and, whoosh! The bike went up like a torch. We only just got off in time!'

This happened in Fulham on the way home, just a short distance from Martin's flat. 'A bus stopped and the conductor rushed over with a fire extinguisher to put it out. I pushed it back to my flat and then went out and got drunk. I came back in the early hours of the morning and saw my poor bike outside the flat and, because I was tight, I thought I would kick it over and see if it would start.

'I switched on the ignition and it all came on, so I thought "Great!" I turned on the petrol and kicked it over, but the fire had burnt all the insulation off the HT leads. Whoomph… the whole lot went up in flames again! I ran into the house and did the worst possible thing – I got a bucket of water and threw that over it – a petrol fire! It spread worse than ever! Luckily, a nightwatchman came out with a fire extinguisher, a very big one and he turned it into a wedding cake!'

The bike was slowly rusting outside when a passer-by stopped and bought it. 'In the end,' Martin said, 'he gave me 13 quid for it and I waved it off down the road. I'd had all that pleasure for just 2 quid.'

He emerged from LAMDA in 1965 full of hopes for the future and soon afterwards headed for his first job with Hornchurch repertory company in Essex where he was taken on as an assistant stage manager. As an ASM, he was essentially the theatre company's general dogsbody and he was paid the princely sum of £7 a week. To save money, he lived for a while in a shed at the bottom of someone's garden where he had an electric ring to cook on and just about nothing else. While some thought his unusual choice of digs was bizarre, others admiringly considered it "Far out, man".

Martin found he could rent the shed for 30 shillings (£1.50) a week, which left him with just over a fiver for food and cigarettes and to buy fellow members of the company a round or two. 'I was 22 before I could afford to buy cigarettes in packets of twenty,' he once recalled.

His hard-drinking lifestyle often brought him close to conflict and he can recall lots of narrow scrapes with violence as a young man in London. However, the worst beating he ever suffered happened in his early twenties – and he can't remember a thing about it. He was attacked by a gang of thugs in a London street, just after he had been to his drama school graduation. He had been drinking with a pal when they were set upon in an unprovoked assault and finished up in hospital.

Martin has a blackout about the whole affair but he assumes he must have fought back because when he came round the next day he found teethmarks on his knees and hands where he must have hit someone. 'All I do know for definite,' he said wryly, 'is that my skull was fractured, my cheekbone was smashed, several teeth were knocked out and I ended up having to have a piece of plastic inserted in my right cheekbone.'

He believes his friend had much more sense – he just fell down and lay there. 'I don't know if we were picked on because I was supposed to be a tough guy,' he said, 'but if that was the case, they soon found out how wrong they were because I lost miserably.' He might look like a bit of a hard man who can handle himself but Martin insists he's really a confirmed pacifist. 'But if it happened again I don't know what I would do. You can be a good pacifist, but you can still fight back!'

If Martin thought Hornchurch Rep was ready to recognise his great potential as an actor and hand him the role of Hamlet straight away, the management had other ideas for their new recruit. The first task he was given was to make an inventory of the company's props. Hornchurch was no different from every other repertory company in that money was always tight and making use of existing props was one way of avoiding unnecessary costs.

'I literally did shovel shit for my first job,' he told one of the authors cheerfully. 'There was a whole new stage management team that had taken over there. I was the assistant stage manager and this new stage manager said, "We have an old prop store at the White Hart and according to my book it has not been opened for 30 years. So let's go and see what's in there and make an inventory." And when we opened it up it was ankle-deep in rat shit. There were rat carcasses all over the place and it was pretty revolting. We had to shovel everything out and I just had to stop and laugh at one point. I realised to my horror that I had done three years at one of the best drama schools in the world and one of my first professional jobs was shovelling shit. Surely after this the only way was up?'

But Martin has never been afraid of hard work and he got busy. Later it was discovered that another props room was flooded with a foot of water and he had to sort out the problem. It wasn't the start he would have chosen to his career as an actor, but he mucked in anyway and cheerfully put such menial tasks down to good experience.

Soon he was to become more involved with the theatre's productions, but still without actually treading the boards and uttering a line. He swept the stage, hung scenery, made the tea and proved himself adept at helping to make props. A request to make a sedan chair in just a matter of hours might have been beyond less enthusiastic ASMs, but taking a lead from his grandfather's skill with tools, Martin managed to knock up a very presentable sedan by the required deadline. It was several months before he progressed to walk-on parts and minor roles. Martin Shaw, professional actor, was on his way.

Further appearances in rep followed and, at one point, he shared digs with another up-and-coming actor by the name of Anthony Hopkins. The two young men became friends and spent many a night staying up into the small hours, discussing the theory and craft of acting over copious drinks.

Martin was learning all the time, and in 1967 he made his first appearance on television playing an Irish revolutionary in a play called *Love On The Dole*. It was the first of several small but varied TV roles in quick succession, at a time when he was also starting to make his mark on the stage. Notably, in October 1968, he played Cliff Lewis in a revival of John Osborne's *Look Back In Anger* at the Royal Court theatre in London opposite Jane Asher, for which he received kind notices.

In 1970 he also appeared at the Lyric theatre in *The Battle Of Shrivings* with Sir John Gielgud who, legend has it, first greeted

Martin with the words: 'You're frightfully handsome – I suppose you're married.' And indeed by now he was.

On New Year's Eve, 1968, Martin had married Jill Allen, a beautiful, slim blonde actress he had fallen in love with. They had been living together for some while and marriage was the next logical step. When they decided to tie the knot, Martin was in the middle of a run of *Look Back In Anger* that had by now transferred to London's Criterion theatre. True to tradition, the show had to go on and soon after the couple had exchanged their vows the groom dashed back to the theatre to appear on stage. Martin's friends all agreed that Jill made a beautiful bride and there were a few million TV viewers who would not disagree. Just two days before she became Mrs Shaw, Jill had been seen on TV in *The Best Pair Of Legs In The Business*.

At first money was tight for the young newly-weds, but as Martin's star began to rise they were able to buy a home of their own, and by 1974 they were living in a tall, sunny late Victorian house in Southgate with Harry, an old English sheepdog and a Volkswagen estate car suited to their expanding family. By then, Martin and Jill had three children: sons Luke and Joe and daughter Sophie.

In 1969, a year after getting married, Martin had gained an important TV break when he joined the cast of *Doctor In The House*, a hugely popular comedy series based on Richard Gordon's books and made by London Weekend Television.

The series arrived on TV screens 15 years after Gordon's novels had first spawned a string of medical joke-and-jape movies beginning with the original *Doctor In The House* in

1954, The films starred a clutch of solid British actors including Dirk Bogarde as young medical student Simon Sparrow, as well as Donald Sinden, Kenneth More, Donald Houston and James Robertson-Justice.

No less than 6 sequels followed: *Doctor At Sea*, which introduced a young French actress called Brigitte Bardot, who would go on to become one of the great screen sex sirens, and then *Doctor In Love, Doctor At Large, Doctor In Distress, Doctor In Clover* and *Doctor In Trouble*. Essentially, these movies were a slightly more sophisticated variation on the *Carry On...* films. They were subtler on innuendo but became increasingly more predictable in settings and situations. As the series of movies progressed, the light comedy became ever more contrived.

Nevertheless, the films proved very popular at the box office, so when Frank Muir became head of comedy at London Weekend (the capital's newly franchised ITV station) in 1968, he was keen to get Richard Gordon's novels successfully adapted for the small screen for the first time. To that end, he employed some fresh young writing talent including Graham Chapman and Graeme Garden, two qualified medical doctors who went on to find fame in *Monty Python's Flying Circus* and *The Goodies* respectively.

For television, the series was updated to reflect the Swinging Sixties. But, as with the original stories written by Richard Gordon, the *Doctor In The House* TV series was set in a fictional medical school of a London hospital, St Swithins, and the high jinks of the medicos mainly involved the chasing of pretty nurses with plenty of bedpan banter and lashings of innuendo about bedside manner.

The show paraded an excellent cast led by Barry Evans, Robin Nedwell and Geoffrey Davies, and Martin joined them as Huw Evans, a Welsh doctor rather fond of his drink. He featured in 3 episodes in a series that went down well with viewers and featured the likes of David Jason and Susan George.

That same year he was also able to demonstrate his versatility by playing Horatio in a TV version of *Hamlet* with Michael Redgrave and John Gielgud, and over the next few years he was able to play a variety of TV roles including a jaded soccer star in a play called *Achilles Heel*. To get fit for the role Martin ran 3 miles a day and had the thrill of running out on to the pitch with professional Fulham players for a five-a-side game.

In parallel with his TV roles, he continued to progress as a stage actor and it was a real feather in his cap when in 1973 he joined the National Theatre, then run by Sir Laurence Olivier. It's not hard to envisage the excitement he must have felt when he was auditioned by the great man himself and given the role of Dionysius in *The Bacchae*. Martin was to appear as the young god Dionysius, son of Zeus, king of the gods, wearing little more than a handkerchief-sized piece of chamois leather and Olivier was extremely concerned that he should look as handsomely god-like as possible. 'Are you working out?' he enquired. 'Well, you ought to – you're not going to be wearing any clothes, you know!' Olivier immediately offered to introduce Martin to the gymnasium where he himself regularly worked out to keep fit. Martin readily signed up and began to put himself through a punishing regime of lifting weights in order to look the part.

He was spurred on by the sight of Olivier himself, then regarded as the world's greatest actor, sweating away while going through his exercises. From that point he resolved to keep on exercising throughout his life.

Olivier was then in the sunset of his career, but Martin could not fail to be impressed by the way he retained his enthusiasm and drive, and still continued to challenge himself rather than resting on his laurels. 'He was fantastic, a proper actor/manager in that he cast and auditioned everybody in his company. He knew everyone and everyone knew him, although it was very clear that he was the boss. He used to come and talk to us in the dressing room at night; it was a magical time.' Though Martin's stint at the National was brief, he also got to appear in Franco Zeffirelli's production of *Saturday, Sunday, Monday* – another worthy addition to his fast-growing acting CV.

CORONATION STREET

'He has a presence and a stillness that you can't teach. He had a silly little part really but he worked hard and made the most of it. We knew he would be a star if he stuck at it'
Coronation Street star Peter Adamson

As a young man, Martin Shaw had enormous sympathy for the hippy movement. Their enthusiasm for free expression and rebellious challenge of authority struck a real chord with him. The ideals of anti-consumerism and resistance to corporate control were close to his heart. So in 1967 when he was invited to play a hippy in *Coronation Street* he was intrigued to say the least.

'I had been working up at Granada on all sorts of drama for a while so I was delighted to get the chance to be in the Street,' said Martin. 'But I was a bit surprised to be told the role was as a hippy – I wasn't aware there were any in Weatherfield!'

But it was an offer he had no intention of refusing and

towards the end of 1967 he walked down the famous cobbles playing the posturing and rather over-confident Robert Croft who arrived with his friends at a New Year's Eve party at Number 11 and flatly refused to leave. Croft announced that he and his 'commune' were taking over the house which alarmed occupant Dennis Tanner, who had been persuaded by early Street wild-child Lucille Hewitt to hold the party. Lucille was very taken with the young revolutionary and a brief affair began. Headstrong Lucille moved in with the group, much to the horror of her guardian Annie Walker.

The legendary pub landlady took immediate action and told property landlord Edward Wormold that her ward had been kidnapped by Devil worshippers. Ruthless Wormold was quick to take action. Dennis was behind with his rent so he quickly received a notice to quit. In a scene which brought many outraged letters of protest from traditional Street fans, the popular Dennis called Annie 'an interfering old cow' and said he would move on with the hippies as Croft and his group prepared to leave, although it was a threat he failed to carry out.

'I was amazed by the professionalism and the team spirit,' said Martin. He was just one of a promising group of young actors that included Kenneth Cranham and John Thaw, who were given a great deal of challenging work in drama productions by Granada. 'We were their young lions,' he recalled fondly later on. 'But part of the price was that you were expected to pay your dues by making an appearance in *Coronation Street*. It was a great deal more enjoyable than I had expected. But I have always been surprised that it is so well remembered by so many people. I was only there for a few weeks but it was a memorable experience and I made some great friends.' He enjoyed several drinking sessions with a number of the cast and most notably recalled time spent with Peter Adamson, who played Len Fairclough. 'He was a real television star and a very nice bloke,' said Martin. 'He showed me that some moments in soap can be just as dramatic and well-acted and directed as in one-off plays or films.'

Adamson later insisted he knew that Martin was destined for greatness as an actor. 'He has all the technical skills you could ever imagine,' he told one of the authors. 'But he has so much more as well. He has a presence and a stillness that you can't teach. He had a silly little part really but he worked hard and made the most of it. We knew he would be a star if he stuck at it.'

But it was after work that the two men really bonded. 'His ability as a drinker was even more impressive than his acting,' smiled Peter. 'I was drinking very heavily then but I always used to feel terrible the next day. Martin would breeze in full of the joys of spring after even the heaviest night. It must have been his youth!'

Martin's short stint had only just ended when a young Liverpudlian actor called Bill Kenwright made his debut in the Street. Bill came in to play Gordon Clegg, who became the show's first pin-up. Martin and Bill became friends and years later their careers would coincide again in even more glittering circumstances.

MACBETH

'Macbeth is a violent play and I've never believed in cop-outs'
Roman Polanski

Towards the end of August 1970, an announcement was made to the press that a new film version was to be made of William Shakespeare's *Macbeth*. The news provoked general excitement among lovers of Shakespeare's great work about the Scottish lord who becomes king through deceit, treachery and 'murder most foul'. But their excitement quickly gave way to apprehension on several counts once it was revealed who was behind the project.

It emerged that the film's backers would be the London arm of Hugh Hefner's Playboy organisation who were making a first foray into film production. The movie would be co-scripted by Kenneth Tynan and Roman Polanski, and the man at the helm for one of literature's grisliest classics would be Polanski himself.

This was the same Hefner who had given to the world the Bunny Girl and an abundance of naked Playmates in his *Playboy* magazine; and this was the same Tynan who had most recently scandalised less liberal sections of the nation by writing *Oh, Calcutta!* – a brazenly full-frontal nude stage sex-romp which many saw as a step too far even for the permissive 1960s. This, too, was the same Roman Polanski, no less, the Pole who had built a reputation for exploring the darker side of human nature in movies like *Repulsion, Cul-de-sac* and *Rosemary's Baby,* in which the said Rosemary chillingly gave birth to a child of Satan.

For many, still fresh in the memory was Polanski's own personal tragedy of the Manson massacre just one year earlier. On Friday 5 August 1969, his beautiful young wife, actress Sharon Tate, had been brutally slain at their California mansion at 10050 Cielo Drive in Beverly Hills, Los Angeles. The crime was all the more horrific for the fact that Sharon was 8 months pregnant at the time. She had been murdered, along with 4 friends, in a savage ritualistic killing by the crazed members of the Charles Manson 'family'. Several of the bodies had been viciously mutilated and the word 'Pig' was smeared in blood across the front door.

One year later, the start of Manson's trial coincided with the announcement of the *Macbeth* movie project and inevitably threw the spotlight on Polanski. He was well aware of what the general reaction would in all probability be to his choosing to make a blood-soaked drama as his first film after the terrible Manson murders. But he figured he was on a hiding to nothing, whatever he did. If he'd chosen to make a comedy, people would equally have asked how he could possibly go for laughs after such horrific events had touched him so deeply.

Hefner, Tynan, Polanski… The track records of this unusual movie triumvirate prompted one newspaper to dub the project '*Oh, Dunsinane!*' and to predict that this new big-screen *Macbeth* would be awash with gore and nudity. 'Yes, there will be nudity,' Polanski conceded when pressed on the subject, 'but not much. Anyone who expects otherwise will be disappointed.'

If that assurance temporarily appeased serious Shakespeare aficionados, Hugh Hefner set the alarm bells ringing again when he promised that fans would experience 'an entirely new interpretation of the line "Lay on, Macduff!"' Despite the fears and misgiving voiced in some educated circles, there wasn't a single actor or actress in Britain who wasn't hoping to catch Polanski's eye as he cast his net for the key roles in the Scottish play – and Martin Shaw was no exception, particularly when the word got around that Polanski was planning to place emphasis on youth and was seeking largely unknowns.

Martin knew one thing for certain: Polanski's pedigree as a film-maker would ensure that his *Macbeth* would be markedly different from any other Shakespearean plays which had previously made the transition from the stage to the cinema. Polanski was by now an A-list director and if the chance to work for him presented itself, he would grab it with both hands.

In 10 years Polanski had come a long way. In the early 1960s he had frequently been dismissed by Hollywood as the stereotypical short – he stood 5 ft 5 in tall – tyrannical European director. But by now he was considered by some to have a stroke of genius when it came to making movies, especially macabre movies.

Polanski had graduated from film school in Lodz, Poland in 1959 and first started to gain limited but important recognition through a series of short films. Then in 1962 he made his first feature film *Knife In The Water* which, significantly, was the first post-war Polish movie not based on a war theme.

In the quirky art film, Polanski conjured up some truly scary moments involving a couple who find themselves out at sea on a sailing boat and in danger from a teenage hitchhiker they have picked up. The movie earned the diminutive director some worthy credibility and he went on to make a horror film parody *The Fearless Vampire Killers*. It was during the filming of this movie that he fell in love with its star, Sharon Tate, and they subsequently married.

Next, he moved over to London to make *Repulsion*, a disturbing tale of madness and alienation that turned out to be a classy, truly horrific psychological drama. Polanski skilfully contrived to build up a tense atmosphere of evil while drawing out a remarkable performance from his young star, French actress Catherine Deneuve, playing a young, sexually repressed beauty who sinks into insanity as loneliness and her fertile imagination take hold.

Polanski's reputation was growing fast, and the following year he rapidly followed up 1965's *Repulsion* with *Cul-de-sac*, a study in kinky insanity. The success at the box office of these two movies earned him an invitation to move to Hollywood to make his first picture for the major American studio Paramount. This was to be *Rosemary's Baby*, a superior film

version of Ira Levin's diabolical chiller novel for which
Polanski himself wrote the screenplay. It starred Mia Farrow
and John Cassavetes, both giving outstanding performances as
a happily married young couple who take a flat in a run-down
New York apartment block. They become involved in
witchcraft and Satanism, and after being prescribed some
strange pre-natal nourishment by a sinister obstetrician,
Rosemary proceeds to give birth to Satan's child.

Polanski's film managed to be frightening without using
explicit gore or violence, relying instead on the blurring of
reality and nightmare. His direction showed a precise sense of
visual composition: 'An evil-smelling tannis-root charm,
disturbing next-door neighbours, a nightmare rape by the
Devil, even innocent puffs of cigar smoke rising up from
behind occupied armchairs bring menace and terror,' was one
assessment. For Polanski, it all made for a cinematic triumph
and it changed Hollywood's perception of him forever.

His career might have taken a different turn but for the
terrible death of his wife. In his grief, his friends urged him to
throw himself into work to try and put the ghastly tragedy
behind him. All, that is, except fellow film-maker Stanley
Kubrick, who counselled him differently, strongly advising him
to go away and do some sports and eventually he'd feel like
'getting out of the room'.

Polanski took his advice and eventually decided his therapy
would be to take a long skiing holiday with friends in
Switzerland. He skied almost every day for 4 months, and it
was on the ski slopes of Gstaad that he had the idea that he
should turn his attentions to *Macbeth*. Ever since he was a

young man in Krakow, he had always dreamed of making a film of a Shakespearean play. Now he had gained great clout as a director, he felt he could seize the moment to achieve his long-held ambition.

Not everyone thought it was a great proposal. Polanski later recalled that when he phoned his agent to tell him about his plans, he sighed: 'What are you doing to me?' And Hollywood was also less than impressed. 'Roman, you know Shakespeare is box office poison,' one high-ranking studio boss rebuked him.

Undaunted, Polanski pressed on. He flew to London, enlisted the help of Ken Tynan in collaborating on a screenplay and secured a loan as pre-production seed money from his friend Victor Lownes, London boss of the Playboy organisation, who eventually also came up with the money to make the movie.

Naturally there was much press speculation as to who would play Macbeth and Lady Macbeth, particularly as Polanski and Tynan wanted to forsake tradition and portray them not as middle-aged but as a good-looking young couple. 'Usually Macbeth is played as an unpleasant bearded chap,' Polanski pointed out, 'and Lady Macbeth as a nagging bitch, and both are middle-aged.'

Tynan was also anxious to dispel the cloak of doom that usually hangs over the couple. 'They don't know they're involved in a tragedy – they think they're on the verge of a triumph predicted by the witches,' Tynan explained. It was his view that in attempting to fulfil the witches' prophecy, they uncovered a dark side to their nature they never knew existed.

The name of Martin Shaw was never seriously considered

for the lead role, but he was nevertheless overjoyed to secure the substantial part of Banquo, even if he was at first somewhat mystified to be chosen to play a high-ranking Scot almost twice his age as well as being father to a teenage son, Fleance. But if Polanski, who had cast Martin after seeing him on stage at the Royal Court theatre, believed he could pull it off, then that was good enough for him. Keith Chegwin was cast as Banquo's boy. 'Cheggers', as he popularly came to be known on TV many years later, was then just into his teens and hoping to build on a career as a successful child actor.

Banquo is a key figure in Shakespeare's plot. He is with Macbeth when they encounter three witches who prophetically hail Macbeth as 'King', but Banquo as 'father of kings to come'. This places the virtuous Banquo firmly in the path of Macbeth's ruthless ambition sparked by the witches' prophesy. On the eve of Macbeth's coronation celebration, Banquo is subsequently murdered upon his friend's command to prevent his sons ever becoming king in the future.

The role placed great responsibility on Martin to deliver. 'I hope it doesn't sound like an ego trip, but I was only 25 at the time and I was playing a burly Scottish general of 40-ish.' he would later reflect. 'To make that work in a Polanski movie of Shakespeare was, I felt, quite an achievement.'

At the end of October 1970, the blue VIP room at the top of the Playboy Club in London's Park Lane, Mayfair was the venue aptly chosen for Polanski to announce the cast of his *Macbeth* to the press. A host of Bunny girls busily ensured that the glasses of the show-business journalists were topped up until Polanski arrived – one hour late.

Jon Finch, a virile-looking young actor whose path would very significantly cross with Shaw's in a few years' time, was unveiled as Polanski's Macbeth. Finch had been hired just a few days previously after Polanski met him on a plane. But what intrigued Martin and the rest of the signed-up actors was that there was no trace of a Lady Macbeth at the launch. Filming in Wales was due to begin on 1 November and she had yet to be cast.

In fact, Polanski had been hoping to sign the American actress Tuesday Weld, but she was balking at appearing in the nude in Lady Macbeth's sleepwalking scene. After she finally turned the role down, the part was offered to another promising young actress but her boyfriend was having none of it. Shooting was already in progress by the time the role was eventually given to Francesca Annis, a 25-year-old beauty who was starting to make a name for herself as an accomplished actress.

Polanski hired her after seeing her in *The Heretic* and, importantly, she understood and readily accepted why she needed to be filmed nude. 'Roman doesn't exploit nudity for its own sake,' she insisted. 'He doesn't go in for pornography. What he says is that in Lady Macbeth's time people simply didn't wear nightdresses so when she got up to sleepwalk she'd have been naked.' It was, Polanski concurred, just part of his drive for an authentic look to the film '... so that people can believe all this actually happened.'

Macbeth was Martin's first film, and the next 16 weeks spent filming under the guidance of perfectionist Polanski proved to be both a sharp learning curve and an eye-opener. This was by far the most fascinating, and certainly the most demanding role of his career as a professional actor to date. It stretched him in all sorts of ways, not least on the back of a horse!

'That's when I learned to ride properly,' he said. 'I thought I could ride already, having taught myself. But the ex-Indian army officer who was my riding instructor for *Macbeth* just took one look at me and said: "Right, no stirrups – just the bridle. A rising trot." Needless to say I couldn't do it; my legs weren't strong enough. I worked with him for 8 weeks and by the end of that time I could ride. It was just as well – when we were shooting we were sometimes in the saddle for 10 hours a day.

'Jon Finch and I became so besotted with the horses that on days when we weren't wanted for filming, we signed on as riding extras.' Polanski was grateful for their willingness to help out. He didn't have a budget that would allow him to hire the large number of extras he felt he needed and in some instances had to resort to plastic dummies to pass muster in the background.

During his time out of the saddle Martin also volunteered to help exercise the horses. 'There were 300 of them,' he said, 'and only 25 handlers. They were fresh and a bit nervy.' Keith Chegwin shared Martin's affection for the horses, even if he did not always see eye to eye with Polanski, especially when Polanski insisted he get back on a horse after he had hurt himself. Of Polanski, Chegwin has said: 'It was weird, I didn't know who he was. Some days he wouldn't turn up and we had horse-riding competitions with the horses that were hanging around.'

Down the years, all manner of superstitions, myths and supposed jinxes have surrounded the staging of *Macbeth* and, once the production had set up in Portmeirion in Wales and filming was under way, Polanski had every good reason to curse the bad luck that traditionally appears to accompany what some superstitious folk will describe only as 'the Scottish play'. There were bad omens even from the very first day, on which a cameraman was nearly killed when a sudden fierce gust of wind blew him into a crevice.

Polanski had deliberately chosen to film in Wales for its natural beauty and, at this late time of year, to take advantage of dark, brooding autumnal skies. But November 1970 proved to be a thoroughly unpleasant month for the director.

In *Roman*, his remarkable book about his life, Polanski recounted the problems he faced while filming *Macbeth* in Wales: 'Portmeirion was almost flooded that fall. It was another case of "Never seen anything like it in twenty years!"

'At first we welcomed the leaden skies and sinister, bizarre-shaped clouds but it wasn't long before we were enveloped in an icy, almost incessant downpour, unable to shoot except during brief intermissions.'

The rain caused chaos, seeping into everything, causing make-up to run, unsticking beards, panicking horses. And when the rain stopped, fog reduced visibility to a few yards. Polanski summed up his despair by writing, 'The weather played havoc with our shooting schedules, which had to be drastically revised. There were times when I felt I was making an underwater epic.'

For a young thesp like Martin, it was an extraordinary

introduction to film-making on the big scale and, anxious to learn as much as he could, he eagerly watched closely as Polanski went about his work and sorted out or circumvented his many problems, not least with the special effects team. Polanski said they were so disaster-prone he nicknamed them 'special defects'. A fog machine exploded, and catapults designed to propel fireballs into Dunsinane Castle either flopped lamely well short or soared dangerously over the castle on to the beach.

There were, however, light-hearted moments, too during filming, notably when Polanski sent Hugh Hefner a short out-take on his birthday – a filmed sequence of three naked, aged witches collectively singing: 'Happy birthday, dear Hef.'

But Martin must have been as alarmed as anyone in the cast when word got around early in the New Year of 1971 that Polanski was in danger of being dismissed. Partly due to the atrocious weather, the film was well behind schedule and over-budget, and the money men were becoming distinctly edgy.

Another director, Peter Collinson, was put on stand-by for this eventuality while Polanski consoled himself with some advice he had once been given by the Austrian-American director Otto Preminger: 'You don't get fired for going over budget – only for being a lousy director.'

Collinson's presence at Shepperton studios, where *Macbeth*'s interior scenes were being shot, was deliberately low-key. Among the backers the fear was that the cast and crew had such a reverential view of Polanski and what he was setting out to achieve that they might refuse to work for another director.

Macbeth was ultimately rescued by Hugh Hefner, who flew

to London to intervene. Hefner agreed to put up the $500,000 Polanski needed to complete the film and in return Polanski offered to give up a third of his fee. As he threw himself into editing his movie, Polanski envisaged the film being given a London launch with a Royal Command Performance in December of 1971. He felt *Macbeth* deserved a British première and he banked on English critics being far more receptive to his film version of a classic Shakespeare play than those in America.

But to his chagrin, the world première was switched to Hefner's Playboy theatre in New York and scheduled for January 1972. Polanski was not best pleased as January tended to be anything but a vintage month at the cinema in America. Past experience showed that Americans tended to stay in after all the Christmas festivities. To make things worse, Polanski found himself embroiled in a battle with the American censors. Quite apart from considering the film too long, *Macbeth*'s American distributors did not want the film released with an X certificate.

This stance forced Polanski into an argument with the ratings board. When he showed them the film, he got the distinct impression they were viewing it not as a film made by a movie director. 'They were looking at it through the filter of my particular predicament,' he said. Moreover, prior to the screening, word had somehow erroneously reached members of the board that Polanski had used many gallons of pigs' blood for the required gore. In fact, the director had cleverly devised a mixture of instant coffee, food colouring, milk and glycerine which more than adequately did the job.

During filming, the cast did not ever get the impression that Polanski was going too far in his powerhouse pursuit of perfectionism and realism. But Francesca Annis has said: 'When we were filming the murder of Macduff's children, he came in and told the set designers: "No, that's not enough blood. It's not really like that," and started throwing it around the set – that made us think.' When a member of the crew then questioned whether too much blood had been splashed on the walls of the set, Polanski reportedly said: 'You didn't see my house in California last summer.'

Eventually Polanski agreed to three cuts in his film. These were scenes that he later conceded had been too explicit. That was enough to secure an R certificate in America, and Martin and everyone else connected with the movie were also relieved when *Macbeth* was given an AA certificate by the British film censor without any problems. It meant that anyone over 14 could see the film unaccompanied, thus ensuring a much wider audience.

Polanski's finished film did not look remotely like the X-rated adventure Hugh Hefner had promised. There were no sex scenes, and only brief nudity with an absence of eroticism. What audiences did get was slaughter on a stark scale, with close-ups of contorted corpses and dismembered body parts, and not just 3 but 60 witches, who were chosen, not unsurprisingly, for their hideous appearance and lack of teeth. If one of Shakespeare's aims was for his play to shock audiences with Macbeth's dastardly deeds, then the Bard himself would not have been disappointed with Polanski's modus operandi.

Predictably, in America the critics had few kind words for

the director's efforts. The movie had an excellent first week at the New York box office but could not maintain the pace and ended up in the red, prompting Hefner to consider future movie ventures very seriously. In England, however, where the film was accorded a charity premiere attended by Princess Anne and a host of Bunny Girls, the critics were more sympathic to what Polanski was trying to achieve and far less obsessed with the Manson murders. Felix Barker's enthusiastic review in the *London Evening News* was even topped off with the headline 'Macbrilliant!'

Certainly, *Macbeth* was one of the most talked-about films of the year even if it didn't set the box office alight and, for Martin Shaw, the role of Banquo was a great career move. He had third billing in a major international movie helmed by a top director at a time when Britain barely had a film industry worthy of the name.

'I'm particularly proud of *Macbeth*, because it was my first film,' said Martin. 'It brought a lot out of me and was very demanding.' In years to come, he was only too happy to talk about the movie during frequent interviews about his role as Doyle in the TV series *The Professionals*. '*Macbeth* had a profound effect on my career,' he told one interviewer. 'I can't think of any other filmmaker I would rather work with than its director Roman Polanski – it was one of the high spots of my career.'

The whole Polanski experience whetted his appetite for working in movies, but a combination of circumstances, bad luck and bad timing meant that he did not build on *Macbeth* in the way he might perhaps have hoped. It should have been a springboard to higher things but instead Martin spent the next 12 months waiting for the phone to ring. He didn't even have an interview, and nothing came his way. For him, it was a confusing and difficult period at a time when he had so many expectations.

'The Polanski thing led to interesting enquiries,' he said, 'and there were two or three extraordinarily "unlucky" occurrences right afterwards. It wouldn't be right to say what they were because other actors were involved. But I was there and I was cast in major films and then, just at the last minute, something happened or somebody changed their minds, or the producer fell out with the director or the money got lost.

'And so I carried on with TV and theatre, and then the British film industry had one collapse after another. Then *The Professionals* came up, and during the time that I was doing *The Professionals*, the British film industry went through one of its periodic revivals. Then, when I finished *The Professionals*, the film industry was flunking again. So it has not been an area where I've had a great deal of success. I've had some, but not enough for me. I would certainly like to have film success but I would like to do it in British films.

'The difficulty with the British film industry is that it is under-funded and nobody helps. The Government doesn't realise what a cultural resource they have in this country; we're the world's worst at cultural recognition. We have got the best technicians in the world and the Americans love to come here and make films because of the quality of our technicians. Steven Spielberg tried desperately to keep EMI open in Elstree because he liked to come here and work.'

Two interesting, and very different, film opportunities which did, however, come his way in the mid-1970s were *The Golden Voyage of Sinbad* and *Operation Daybreak*.

The latter was directed by Lewis Gilbert, a veteran of several notable war movies including *Reach For The Sky* and *Carve Her Name With Pride*, as well as the James Bond film *You Only Live Twice*. Gilbert returned to his war film roots to make *Operation Daybreak*, based on a true story of a secret mission to assassinate maniacal German commander, Reinhard Heydrich, whom the Nazis had positioned in the Czechoslovakian capital of Prague. Allied intelligence feared that if Hitler should be toppled, Heydrich would continue the expansion of the Third Reich.

Martin, enjoying second billing to American actor Timothy Bottoms, played the duplicitous Czech ex-patriot Sgt. Karel Curda, one of three parachutists sent in to perform Operation Daybreak – the assassination of Heydrich at any cost. But the mission runs into trouble when Martin's turncoat character switches from Allied spy to Nazi informer, in the process giving away details of the location of the headquarters of the Czech liberation movement.

As with Polanski, Martin learned a great deal under Gilbert's measured direction and attention to detail as they filmed in the depths of winter in Prague for three months in 1974. Czechoslovakia was then still a frontline Soviet state and Martin and his fellow cast members were put up in the Alcron hotel, which had been the Gestapo headquarters in the World War II. They were given little chance to explore the magnificent city and, for Martin, seeking out vegetarian fare was far from easy. He discovered there was not even a word for vegetarian in the Czech language. 'It was incredibly difficult to find anything to eat other than pickles, processed cheese and bread,' he later recalled.

But it was a very different story when Martin returned to Prague some 25 years later to film *The Scarlet Pimpernel*. With thousands of Americans now living in the city, he was not observed with suspicion on his shopping expeditions to seek out vegetarian food. 'Vegetarianska' was by now a word in common use. Even so, he was not taking any chances and he carefully packed away some appropriate food and clothes for the three months he expected to be filming on location. When he landed in Prague, however, his luggage went missing for four days and during that time he had no change of clothes or a toothbrush – and, to make matters worse, finding acceptable food was still something of a challenge.

One night while he was in Prague filming *Operation Daybreak*, he picked up the book *Heart of the Hunter* by Laurens van der Post, the South African educator, explorer, conservationist, philosopher and humanitarian. Since the 1950s, van der Post had become well known for his advocacy of the Kalahari desert and the culture of the Bushmen in southwestern Africa and Martin was captivated by his descriptions of the magical properties of the desert where you can 'hear the light'.

The author's prose captured his imagination and he was dreaming of visiting just such a place when the telephone rang with a call offering a star part in *Burke and Wills* to be made in the Australian desert by the BBC. This was an episode for a documentary series called *The Explorers* which used actors to portray the lives of famous adventurers. Soon afterwards, he found himself leaving behind the Prague winter to film in Alice Springs where it was a sweltering 120 degrees Fahrenheit in the shade. 'Only there was no shade, but everything van der Post had said was true,' he commented. 'I was overwhelmed by the beauty of the desert and its purity. You can feel the life force.'

Burke and Wills followed the fanciful and awful story of the journey made in 1860 by legendary Aussie explorers Robert O'Hara Burke and William John Wills. The two men set out on their ill-fated expedition after the government of South Australia offered a prize to the first expedition to cross the Australian continent from south to north.

Martin was cast as Burke, an Irishman who had emigrated to Melbourne and joined the police force, and who eventually died of starvation in 1861. The film was shot in Australia's glorious outback and directed by Lord Snowdon, erstwhile stills photographer Tony Armstrong-Jones, who was then best known as the husband of Princess Margaret.

As Martin was just about the only Englishman in the cast alongside a bunch of Australian actors and film crew, Martin and Tony – as Lord Snowdon preferred everyone to call him – enjoyed a natural affinity and developed a close friendship throughout the duration of the shoot. Martin found him to be a warm, sensitive and intensely private man, and enjoyed working with him.

It was far from easy filming in such sweltering heat. Among cast and crew there were some tetchy moments but Snowdon managed to keep the production moving forward and happy, and ultimately to do the story justice. At first there was some resentment in Australia's acting fraternity that Pommie Martin should star in a film based on such quintessential Aussie explorers, but as the camera rolled, the Pom won them round with his dedication to his work as the cameras rolled.

The Golden Voyage Of Sinbad, filmed in and around Mallorca with a screenplay by Brian Clemens, creator of *The Professionals*, could hardly have been more different from *Operation Daybreak*. This was an adventure story told with some opulence about Sinbad the Sailor coming across a golden tablet, which turns out to be one third of a puzzle.

Martin played Rachid, Sailor Sinbad's first officer, but with limited opportunity for him, as it was John Philip Law as Sinbad and Tom Baker (later to become TV's Doctor Who) as Koura the wizard who caught the eye, as well as the clever tricks of co-producer and special effects artist Ray Harryhausen.

TRANSFORMATION

'The very next day I threw out all the meat from the freezer and became a vegetarian'
Martin on his dramatic change of lifestyle

M artin Shaw thought it was just a happy piece of good fortune when he met up with an old friend from drama school on the set of Roman Polanski's *Macbeth*, but it was a reunion that was to completely change his life. The friend in question was Luke Hardy. Like Martin he was a gifted young actor, but one who had become disillusioned by the profession and thought he had given up acting for good. A devoted follower of the Indian guru Charan Singh, until he met Martin Shaw, Luke had absolutely no idea why he had taken a small part in the film. 'And when he saw me at the studio he knew why he had accepted one more role,' says Martin. Luke realised that although Martin did not know it yet himself, deep down he was not happy with his wild and heavy-drinking lifestyle, inside he was crying out for a direction in his life.

They had originally become close as young men at drama school. 'We used to drink and womanise a lot together,' said Martin frankly. The two men talked and talked, and Martin saw that Luke had found the sort of calm inner peace that he himself had been unconsciously searching for. Much later, Martin explained the significance of the meeting to writer Garth Pearce: 'Intellectually I don't know what made me get involved in the first place, but spiritually it was my time. Back then I was drinking heavily, sometimes up to a bottle of whisky a day, and I was also a stone overweight and eating all sorts of meat. When the time was right... that was it.' Charan Singh was a living yogi whose teachings had given Luke Hardy a sense of purpose and a real meaning to his life. 'In a nutshell his belief is to go back to God while you are still alive rather than have to wait until you die,' said Martin.

The friends talked long into the night, and Luke told Martin everything he had learned about clean living and vegetarianism. Straight away, these ideas began to have an effect on him. Cutting out the meat from his diet was the first decision. 'The very next day I threw out all the meat from the freezer and the Oxo and the Bovril and became a vegetarian.' And it was largely on moral grounds – with the passion of the converted, Martin was quickly asking questions like: 'How can you justify hacking off a little lamb's leg or ripping out a pig's belly just because you like the taste?' Also, to his relief he soon felt noticeably fitter: 'All this talk about needing the protein meat provides just did not seem true in my case.'

Giving up alcohol took rather longer. 'Over the next 12 months I read everything I could get my hands on about what Luke and I had talked about,' said Martin. 'Gradually, very slowly, I became a convert. Doubts kept coming my way – "A man can't be a God," "What about the other bad things that happen in the world?" But every single question I threw at Luke got answered.'

Inside a year he also went from being a heavy drinker to a teetotaller. From the first time he started to sneak halves of bitter as a 14-year-old schoolboy, Martin had always enjoyed alcohol. 'I liked the taste of booze,' he said. 'That was part of it, and as your resistance builds up so does the amount you need to make you feel relaxed.' At drama school, he was at the centre of a hard-living group and he admitted that at one point his daily diet included a bottle of whisky, two bottles of wine and several pints of Guinness. He knew he had gone way past simple social drinking; he was hitting the bottle and hitting it hard. Living in a flat in London he was really putting the pints away and he put on a couple of extra stones in weight. 'Young actors have a lot of time to drink,' said Martin. 'You might be on in the evening in a stage play but that leaves you all day to drink. It got so I was starting in the morning with whisky when sensible people were having a cup of tea.

'What started as a game became serious drinking. People wanted to be like Peter O'Toole, Richard Burton and Oliver Reed. It was terribly glamorous to demonstrate that you were gritty and real by being unshaven, to smell of alcohol and be unpredictable. Of course,' he said years later, 'nothing is more predictable than going around unshaven, smelling of alcohol and shouting at everyone.

'When I did the revival of *Look Back In Anger* at the Royal Court there was a quiz in the *Guardian* saying, "If you answer 'Yes' to any of the following ten questions you are probably an alcoholic". I had to answer 'Yes' to three of them. I would drink anything – Scotch and wine during the show and the same afterwards. I was not moderate in any way; the only purpose of alcohol was to get drunk.'

Meeting friends at lunchtime involved more alcohol, and in terms of units he was way into the danger area. In fact Martin was warned by his doctor to give up drink because it was endangering his health, but he took no real action until his inspirational meeting with Luke Hardy. 'Part of the realisation that the teachings of Charan Singh made a difference for me was stopping drinking,' he said. 'Once I had come to the conclusion that his way was the right way for me, I came to totally reassess my life. I began to realise that drink was poisoning my mind as well as my body.' Not drinking meant no longer going into pubs, which he described with a smile as 'another welcome side effect of Charan Singh's guidance.'

But Martin possesses a fierce determination and when he makes a decision he sticks by it with a passion. When he finally decided to stop drinking, he did it instantly. 'I was in a pub having a pint of Guinness,' he recalled. 'And I thought, "This will be the last one."'

The meeting with Luke Hardy was in 1971 and it made a profound enough impact on him for Martin to name his first son after his friend. 'It changed everything for me,' he said.

'Nothing was ever quite the same again. Luke started a small clothing business in 1972. A bale of clothing arrived at London Airport and Luke's sister suggested he sell it. I used my car to go and collect it. We took it around a few boutiques. And from that small beginning grew a successful business, with shops all over the place. Luke stayed outside acting; he thought it did not match with his beliefs.'

In addition, meditation became an important part of his life. 'I meditate for two hours in the morning and half an hour at night,' he said. 'There is a meditation which has a purely physical benefit to take your mind away from the strains and stresses of the day, then there is the kind which is a discipline to give you spiritual advancement. But that is the sort of spiritual advancement that comes from within, to gain power and to go further up.

'The path that I follow says that you do not have to wait until you are dead to go beyond. You can do it while you are alive. I have to make it very clear that what I tell you now about meditation is what I have learned, but not experienced. One of the vows that we take is that you should never, ever reveal what has happened to you during meditation, otherwise it would be impossible to separate what you are saying from ego. All the people who follow the path that I do never ever talk about meditation. What happens is that as you develop over the years, your concentration grows for you to vacate your body, which is when you step into, literally, other planes of existence. Yogis have done this for thousands of years. The problem with that is, as soon as you get out of your physical body, the very first step – horizontally – you are in a creation and existence that is a million times more attractive than this one.

'A lot of the great yogis get stuck on the first or second plane. As I said, I follow a living yogi, Charan Singh. The purpose of having a living master is that you can see him and know what his vibe is like. When he initiates you he implants his radial form, his astral body, at your eye centre. I know how this must sound but, believe me, I have studied it for a long time. He has already made the journey from the body to another plane and when you start to have success in meditation there are so many negative things going on inside. The great benefit of having a master – who you love like the disciples of Christ did – is that you see him on the outside and the inside; you keep on following him upwards and upwards.

'I go to group meetings and there are old ladies, skinheads, hippies, bank clerks, actors, musicians... It is a total cross-section of people. Master is very understanding. The way you were born is how you are. Luke thought acting was a distraction. What happened was that his business became huge. I did not have the remotest idea that I would go in for all this. Nothing could have been further from my mind at the time.'

And there were more practical benefits from his new life as well. 'Through meditation I heard about the wild-flower remedies,' said Martin. 'Did you know there are 38 different kinds of herbs for treating states of mind like jealousy, anger and irritation?'

He is well aware that his wide-eyed enthusiasm can sometimes provoke ridicule but he knew he was in for a sympathetic hearing when he told his father all about his beliefs. After all, he already knew that his relentless quest for truth and discovery was inherited. 'He really listened,' said Martin. 'Most people when they first hear about it either go glassy-eyed or cynically go, "Ah Ha!", which I might well have done myself a few years before. But my dad listened and I spouted for about an hour and a half, and he said, "You know I believe I have been looking for that for 40 years." It was a wonderful moment between us.'

Visitors to Martin Shaw's dressing room have remarked on the gold-framed colour photograph of Charan Singh on his table. The beaming face of the guru is topped by a white turban and he proudly wears a long grey beard and a benevolent smile. Martin refers to Charan Singh simply as 'the man who changed my life' or 'my spiritual healer'. He sincerely believes he was well down the road to self-destruction when he met Luke Hardy. His belief in the teachings of Charan Singh completely refocused his life. 'It is a path I have followed ever since,' he says.

He sees no reason to be embarrassed or awkward about his devotion. In fact, he has many times tried to explain his motivations to a wider public despite knowing perfectly well that he could easily be misinterpreted and come out sounding like a complete crackpot.

In many ways, Martin Shaw is a very private person yet he went to great pains in an interview with journalist Ian Woodward to try to spell out exactly why he draws such strength from his beliefs. He said: 'There is a place or a person or a thing or an entity, which everyone knows by different names, like God or the Lord or whatever, and at one time there was just that and nothing else. And then, for reasons best known to itself/himself/whatever – if you imagine that thing as an ocean then drops separated from it, and that was the first action, and every action has an opposite reaction, so that produced more and more reactions. These drops went through various stages, various altered states, and got further and further away from their source until they became Mind, and from Mind they became astral plane, until they finally crystallised into steam, water and ice; this is in turn crystallised into a physical form and became very dense and very coarse. The essence of the ocean of the Lord is still within every human being, is still here. It's what makes people restless, what makes people lonely, what makes people fall in love. It's just a reflection of the love for the Lord that they once had.

'What keeps people bound in the body is the cycle. Now in the West all this sounds like nonsense, yet 85 per cent of the world's population believe in karma and in reincarnation; it's only in the West that we don't have very much knowledge of it. The purpose of this path is not to make life easier, although one of the side effects is that it does make life easier. The real purpose is to enable me to get out of this life altogether and not have to return in a human body. I've never acknowledged that before and maybe it's time I told the absolute truth about what I'm doing so that the public can learn what kind of nutcase I really am! The purpose of this path for me is to finish off all my karma residual attachment to a physical plane, make a hasty retreat and never come back to it again. Now the only way you can do that is to be guided and taken through the journey inside you by somebody who knows that "inside" way

– Charan Singh. He has taught me the calming effect of meditation. His presence alone is inspirational and I have met him several times. His whole philosophy of life is to do with love and integrity. This is why I am a vegetarian.'

Though the changes in Martin were remarkable, not quite all his predictions at that time came true. He said in 1982 that in 10 years, or hopefully 5, he wanted to be out of show business altogether, he planned at the time to switch track and run some kind of pioneering healing institute where he could use all the knowledge of alternative medicine and herbalism that he had built up. 'Although I love my job as an actor,' he said, 'and although I am artistically dedicated to it, I don't feel as attached to it as I once did. To be honest, and I have not said this publicly before, I can see that my spiritual and emotional attachment is being directed much more towards healing. That's where my heart lies.'

Martin's encounter with his old friend Luke in the 1970s changed his life completely. He became much more self-aware and determined to behave as well as possible in all circumstances. Martin admitted he had a temper and he realised in future he would always do his utmost to control it. 'The change in my personality has been gradual,' he said. 'But I believe my beliefs have made me more tolerant, a lot more loving and generally more understanding.'

HELEN: A WOMAN
OF TODAY

*'I was arrogant, just like Frank Tulley. I pushed people about so
much I couldn't keep a secretary for more than a few weeks'*
Martin on his role as a faithless husband in *Helen: A Woman Of Today*

ITV's 1973 drama series *Helen: A Woman Of Today* was
supposed to make a star of actress Alison Fiske. She played
the none-too-glamorous cheated wife and mother who
bravely decides to divorce her lying husband Frank after he has
an affair with a pretty blonde. Only it didn't quite turn out like
that. Almost as if to prove that there is no justice in the world
and to confound the emerging feminist movement, the series
helped to provide a launch pad for Martin Shaw, even though
he played feckless Frank from behind a moustache that looked
like a droopy dormouse.

Frank was certainly not the sort of character to impress
Martin. After the production of the 13-week series was over
the actor was left feeling absolutely exhausted, partly, he said,

because Frank was so completely different from himself. He hated him. 'Frank is the quintessence of male pride,' he said. 'I despise this sort of man. I wouldn't like him if he was simply over-masculine, but this is a cover for weak mindedness. When he gets involved in this stupid business with another woman he fails to deal with the situation. He lies to her and his wife. He plays the odds like a mad gambler. It is mentally and physically debilitating to work on a long series – even more so when the person you're playing is like Frank.'

Martin felt strongly that Frank Tulley was a classic male chauvinist. After filming he said: 'I disagreed with everything he stood for, so I played him as realistically as possible. The way I see it is that both sexes deserve equal opportunities and equal respect, although they both have a different role to play.' He insisted he felt that to put a woman down or treat her badly just because she is a woman is just as wrong as treating someone badly because they happen to be black, or Jewish, or gay, or disabled. Of course, women still have babies though, he pointed out, and said he believed that it was just as stupid for women to deny their womanhood as it was for men to try to force them to be something they're not. 'Men are sometimes restricted by their masculine roles, too,' said Martin. 'I would hate to have to be strong all the time.'

In fact the series almost never got made. Television producer Richard Bates, the son of famous writer H E Bates, saw it as the follow-up to *A Man of Our Times*, which had been a great success some five years earlier, and starred George Cole struggling through a crisis in his life. Bates believed that defiant Helen would strike a chord with all the millions of independent women who were then busy reading *Spare Rib* and copies of Germaine Greer's *The Female Eunuch*, but almost everyone turned down the show before London Weekend Television decided to give it a try. Brilliant director Jim Goddard took control and somehow the series produced reactions that no one had predicted.

At first, Martin was happy to be the bad guy of the piece as, after the shock of discovering his infidelity, conventional middle-class Helen strove to study and build a new life for herself and their two young children. Many male viewers, including a few influential critics, decided that Helen was a little too strident and sorry for herself. Her awkwardness, it was argued, was at least partly responsible for Frank's fling with a temptress tantalisingly played by Sharon Duce. After all, Frank did at one point come home with his tail between his legs and, from somewhere behind his alarming moustache, muttered that he was sorry. He said he loved her and their two children, and asked for another chance. Helen was widely advised to swallow her pride and take him back, but she refused.

Martin did not agree with the viewers who had decided Frank was hard done by; he believed his character had brought it all on himself. And he went on to describe Frank as a symptom of the sickness that was troubling the whole world at that time. He condemned him as a man swept up by a competitive, dissatisfied society, who sacrifices his family unit in the interests of a new sexual experience. Martin said at the time, when he was just 28 years old, that in the values of the day he himself felt like a misfit, telling the *TV Times* magazine: 'I dwell in the past. There is nothing I like about the present. I am constantly taking my mind back to the filthy streets in Birmingham where I grew up. Things seemed to move so much slower then. All we have now is overcrowded roads, ugly buildings, noise, and no concern for others. Frank Tulley is a perfect piece of that rat-race jigsaw.'

Martin even recognised aspects of Frank in his previous life. After leaving school, in his job as a sales clerk with a chemical firm, he had pushed himself forward to take charge of the advertising department. 'I was arrogant, just like Frank Tulley,' he said.

A STREETCAR
NAMED DESIRE

'I finally decided the role was a size too large for me'
Marlon Brando on being asked to play
Stanley Kowalski in *A Streetcar Named Desire*

In late 1973 Martin Shaw was filming *The Golden Voyage Of Sinbad* in Spain when an urgent telephone call came through. It was his agent informing him that there was an important stage role in the offing. He knew at once that the play was *A Streetcar Named Desire*, the co-star was to be Claire Bloom and the role on offer was Stanley Kowalski.

Martin needed a couple of hours to think about it. He would be stepping into a role made famous by Marlon Brando, first on Broadway in 1947 and then in the movie that followed. Twenty-three years had elapsed since the movie version of Tennessee Williams' play, but the name Kowalski was still synonymous with Brando's. With a single role, Brando had changed the whole nature of acting in America and Martin

69

wondered how he could possibly erase that iconic performance from the minds of a theatre audience in a new version of *A Streetcar Named Desire*. His first instinct therefore was to dismiss the idea, but he subsequently changed his mind when his agent told him he would be mad not to go for it.

Ironically, Brando himself had done precisely the same thing when asked to play Kowalski, turning the part down by saying: 'I finally decided the role was a size too large for me.' Instead of needing just two hours, however, Brando required a week before he acquiesced and then proceeded to electrify the theatrical world with a stunning performance that was hailed as a landmark in American theatre.

Brando had the audience at the Ethel Barrymore Theatre in New York on their feet and cheering on the opening night on Wednesday, 3 December 1947, and he proceeded to excite packed houses in the same role for the next two years. When the naturalism that he had created on stage was later preserved on film in a superbly detailed performance, it would influence a whole generation of actors. The Marlon mumble and his Method acting meant that film acting would never be the same again after the movie version of *A Streetcar Named Desire*. Tennessee Williams' story was screenplayed into an even more absorbing drama of frustration and stark tragedy, with Vivien Leigh as the morally disintegrated Blanche Dubois, a role originated on Broadway by English-born actress Jessica Tandy.

It was, however, somewhat to Martin's advantage that he had never seen the film and could therefore embark on the role of Kowalski with no preconceived ideas. He approached it from his own observations of the script. Kowalski has a lot of animal magnetism, he decided, and a total lack of self-doubt. 'According to Tennessee Williams, the animal joy of being exudes from every pore,' he deduced.

Martin was an actor who didn't believe in auditions – he felt they could never really convey to a director what an actor was capable of. However, for *A Streetcar Named Desire* he submitted to a sight-reading and, when he'd finished, the director asked him to take his shirt off. 'Christ, you look like a chicken!' he exclaimed. 'Can you do anything about it?' And so Martin took himself off to a gym to work on weights to give himself a brawnier look more suited to the kind of swaggering, self-assured brutish, challenging Kowalski.

When the play opened in March 1974, with Joss Ackland and Morag Hood also added to the cast, it was to Martin's credit that the audience was enormously responsive to his portrayal and he garnered encouraging reviews and no little praise for rising above the memory of Brando.

Writer Helen Dawson, who caught the play on its second night, had this to say about Martin Shaw: 'It is a performance of considerable brute force. Mr. Shaw, unlike many English actors, is not afraid to let go and, at times, he can make the theatre quake.'

Martin was ecstatic and confessed to driving around Piccadilly Circus just to stare at his name up in big neon lights alongside that of such a leading actress as Claire Bloom. He was pleased with his performance and, he has said, it was the first time that he began to feel that he might be any good as an actor. But it was also scary for him knowing that now he had gained that sort of stature he would have to make sure he deserved it.

Some 14 years later he reprised the role in Brisbane and Sydney, Australia, where, to keep himself toned for the role, he set up mini-gyms in the flats he was renting.

THE PROFESSIONALS

'So there you have them. Doyle and Bodie. The Bisto Kids.
The Terrible Two. The Team. Black & Decker. Marks & Spencer.
Nitro & Glycerine'
Brian Clemens, creator of *The Professionals*

By 1977, Martin Shaw could feel thoroughly satisfied with
the way his career was going. But then came the series
that was to change his life in a way he could scarcely have
thought possible. The first half of the 1970s had seen a plethora
of police and secret agent series successfully launched on TV,
including *Department S, Mission Impossible, The Protectors, Van der
Valk, The Sweeney* and *The New Avengers.* Then, in 1976, came
the American import *Starsky And Hutch,* a cop show about two
Los Angeles police pals starring former daytime soap actor Paul
Michael Glazer as dark-haired, junk-food-eating, streetwise
Starsky and fair-haired David Soul as the health-food-eating,
quieter half of the two.

Together they brought the tradition of the action-packed 'buddy' movie to TV, laced with a liberal helping of fraternalistic pals-for-life sentimentality between the two main characters. At the very beginning the tone of each episode was set with scenes of police cars crashing through piles of cardboard boxes and the fearless duo diving and sprawling on to the bonnets and roofs of cars in their relentless pursuit of criminals.

The show proved to be a big weekend hit for the BBC, so much so that, extraordinary to relate in hindsight, it even spawned a fad for chunky belted cardigans for men, as worn by Starsky. Over on ITV, the 15 commercial channels were countering the crimebusting action of *Starsky And Hutch* with the independently-produced series *The New Avengers* starring Joanna Lumley, Gareth Hunt and Patrick Macnee, the latter reprising his original role of bowler-hatted Steed from *The Avengers*.

But problems were starting to arise with the French and Canadian financial backing for *The New Avengers* and it was clear that the show would soon have to end. It prompted ITV's big 5 companies – Thames, Granada, ATV, Yorkshire and London Weekend – to search for a successor.

London Weekend, who were taking a hit in the ratings from *Starsky And Hutch*, were especially keen to match them and Brian Tesler, LWT's programme controller, summoned British screenwriter Brian Clemens and asked him to come up with a 'new, fast-moving show that related to the seventies.' Tesler could hardly have looked to a better man to create the kind of show he was seeking. Clemens' track record was exemplary. He had gained his big break by writing the pilot script for *Danger Man*, a popular series starring Patrick McGoohan as an internationally famous security investigator whose services were available only to governments or highly placed government officials. Clemens then proceeded to prove his pedigree after Syd Newman, head of drama at Associated British Corporation (ABC) television came up with the title *The Avengers* and told him: 'I don't know what the hell it means, but it's a good title, so now go and write something that fits it.'

Clemens did just that and came up with a fantasised espionage drama that was first broadcast in 1960 and became one of the biggest hit television series of all time. *The Avengers* was seen all over the world, has frequently been repeated, and still pulls in sizeable audiences to this day, fully 45 years since its inception.

Clemens not only wrote and produced *The Avengers*, but he was also responsible for its stylised pop visuals and tongue-in-cheek approach. Importantly for Tesler, Clemens was used to working to tight schedules – he turned out a new episode of *The Avengers* in just 10 days. Tesler knew he would deliver and sent Clemens off to his typewriter indicating he wanted a buddy show but something that had considerably more bite than *Starsky And Hutch*.

Clemens went away and committed two ideas to paper. His first was for a series about two undercover cops, and the second was a series he provisionally called *The A Squad* about an elite force formed to tackle a wide-range of villainy and outrage including terrorism, hijackings, bomb threats, hostage-taking, kidnapping, espionage, gun-running, racketeering and organised crime. *The A Squad* had the advantage of international appeal, and this was an important consideration for Clemens. He wanted to create a series that was not tailored just to the UK but would also sit well in the world market.

Ten days at his typewriter later, Clemens was back to put his proposals to Tesler, who expressed real interest in *The A Squad*, but with one reservation – he didn't like the title. It just wasn't commercial enough, he said. In his proposal for *The A Squad*, Clemens outlined his idea of an elite force called CI5 (Criminal Intelligence 5), a 40-strong body of specialists drawn from all the forces and services, and controlled from offices within the Home Office.

In charge would be George Cowley, a well-respected former MI5 veteran with a clear mission: 'Our job is to see that no one craps on *our* doorstep, and that means preventative detection, preventative action,' Clemens wrote. 'It's no good the girl taking the Pill *after* the boozy weekend, and the same applies to us. You're the Bisto Kids – you get the slightest whiff of anything and you move in – shake 'em down, crush 'em before they even *start* to grow.' The squad would not be afraid to meet violence with violence to save the innocent.

Clemens envisaged the series concentrating on Cowley and two of his top enforcers who worked as a team. He named them Ray Doyle and William Bodie. Fleshing out the duo's respective backgrounds for Brian Tesler, he decided that Doyle was fair-haired, had a touch of Gaelic about him, and his handsome face had a deceptively gentle look to it. 'It's those blue eyes really, they have a lazy, dreamy way of looking at you – just before he hits you,' he wrote.

As for Doyle's background, Clemens decided he was a Londoner who had first worked in a shop and studied art in the evenings before joining the police then rapidly becoming an outstandingly good detective. Now he worked for CI5, 'and if anyone in that amoral organisation has leanings towards a morality, it's Ray Doyle.' In almost every way Bodie was a contrast to Doyle – a dark-haired former merchant seaman who became a soldier and was a first-class shot with a rifle. Unlike Doyle, Bodie was bristling with aggression and together they made a crack team.

Clemens finished his proposal with the following writing brief: 'Set up the story, set up the problem CI5 have to deal with – and then let's see how they solve the apparently insoluble. Keep the relationship of Doyle and Bodie – with Cowley – firmly in the foreground. Steal situations from the headlines. No situation must suspend belief.' Clemens signed off his brief: 'Keep it moving. Fast.'

Tesler was impressed and enthusiastic enough about the concept to commission a script from Clemens with the promise that if he liked it, London Weekend Television would make a 13-part series. He was as good as his word and allocated a budget of £115,000 for each episode with a view to production beginning in the summer of 1977. The show would be re-named *The Professionals* and would be produced independently for LWT.

Jon Finch, the good-looking young actor who had, of course, starred alongside Martin Shaw's Banquo in Polanski's *Macbeth*, was the preferred choice to play Doyle. When auditioned, Finch professed to be keen to take on the role, but not long afterwards Clemens and his creative partner Albert Fennell were astonished to be confronted by their star declaring: 'Of course, I can't possibly play an ex-policeman.' They were flabbergasted by his protestation, not least because they believed Finch had read the script and had therefore made himself thoroughly familiar with the format and Doyle's characterisation before professing his eagerness to play Doyle.

Reluctantly, Clemens and Fennell went back to square one and proceeded to audition dozens of other young actors with the required virile appeal and Martin Shaw emerged as their top choice. Shaw had impressed Clemens when he appeared in an episode of *The New Avengers* playing the curiously named Larry Doomer, a former boyfriend of Purdey (Joanna Lumley), who was out to kill an Arab she had been hired to protect.

When he was offered the role of Doyle, Martin had little hesitation in accepting. The series had a good pedigree in Clemens and Fennell, it had the weight of London Weekend Television behind it, and he would be paid a reasonable fee of £400 an episode.

Martin was also confident that his track record as an actor who had an ability to play a wide range of roles would be good enough to prevent him from being typecast. But he hadn't reckoned on the Press and their determination to give him a 'TV tough-guy' tag, something he would find irksome for years to come.

Once Martin was in place to play Doyle, he was required to screen-test alongside several other actors in a bid to find another who would gel with him enough to become his on-screen partner Bodie. Clemens eventually settled on Anthony

Andrews, an actor whom Martin already knew well from the film *Operation Daybreak* in which, like Martin, he had had a substantial supporting role. The two young men had got on well during the filming of *Operation Daybreak*. They liked each other and, importantly, respected each other's dedicated approach to acting. Martin knew he could work well with Andrews and was delighted when their screen test together met with the approval of Clemens.

But when Clemens reviewed the rushes after some preliminary filming, he instantly felt 'trepidation' that the partnership simply wasn't working. There was something about the Shaw-Andrews combination that made him feel uneasy. He had committed to Andrews, but in the end he reckoned that together the two actors simply didn't have the sparky rapport he was looking for, perhaps because they were too alike – and perhaps too matey. 'They tended to sit in the car and giggle,' a worried Clemens noted. There was nothing for it but to go with his gut instinct. Andrews, he decided, would not be playing Bodie after all.

For Andrews, this change of heart came as a huge shock and it was a decision that was also greeted by Martin with acute disappointment. At the time, it must have been a bitter blow for the actor to have such a major role snatched away from him just when he had one arm through Bodie's shoulder holster. Looking back, however, Andrews might well regard it as a blessing in disguise, given the career constrictions that the series was later to place on Martin, and given that he himself was able to go on and become an international star with *Brideshead Revisited* – eventually winning a BAFTA Best Actor award for his performances as the dissolute drunken Sebastian Flyte.

Yet more auditions failed to find the right partner for Martin until Brian Clemens remembered Lewis Collins, a young man who had coincidentally also appeared in the same 'Obsession' episode of *The New Avengers* as Martin. He recalled that the two had not particularly got on; there had been limited interplay between their respective characters, '...but when we did, it was fairly abrasive,' Martin later reported enigmatically.

Fittingly and prophetically, however, Lewis Collins' character in *The New Avengers* delivered a line to Martin's character, Doomer, in which he ventured: 'Maybe we should work together again?' Little did he know how meaningful that line was to become.

Up to that point, Collins' most notable TV appearance had been in the ITV comedy *The Cuckoo Waltz* as Gavin Rumsey, an archetypal girl-chasing medallion man who became the lodger of a newly married couple played by Diane Keen and David Roper.

Lewis' masculine good looks had proved popular with female viewers of *The Cuckoo Waltz* in his role as flash bird-puller Gavin and, when placed alongside Martin, Clemens felt there was just that hint of an edge between the two that he was looking for. He was duly signed to play Bodie.

Born and raised in Liverpool, Lewis Collins was the first to concede he was a very different animal from either suave Anthony Andrews, or for that matter Martin Shaw. He had grown up in Birkenhead, a rough, tough area of the city, where he had to look after himself with his fists when occasion demanded. He counted himself lucky because instead of becoming mixed up with teenage gangs and getting into trouble, Lewis got into girls early and he would regularly head for the cinema with a girlfriend of his choice, especially on Sunday afternoons when the new week's film came around.

The movies and TV had enthralled him, he says, right from the time as a small boy he first saw *The Range Rider*, an American kids' western TV series screened in the early 1950s. He thrilled to the adventures of 6-foot 4-inch former stuntman Jock Mahoney who, with his youthful sidekick, roamed all over the old frontier, righting wrongs and helping out everyone from Arizona Navajos to Canadian Mounties, with all his good deeds of course accomplished with athletic stunts.

'Later, of course, when all the Liverpool groups were starting, including some outfit called The Beatles, my girlfriends and I started going to the clubs as well as the cinemas,' he said. Watching Liverpool's raw beat combos – The Beatles, The Searchers, The Swinging Blue Jeans, Rory Storm and the Hurricanes, The Merseybeats and Gerry and the Pacemakers – performing at local venues like the famous Cavern club and winning recording contracts fired Lewis's own musical ambitions. He saw the excitement they all generated and that there was money to be made; he wanted a part of it.

His father wanted Lewis to be a drummer in a band, but he himself preferred to buy a bass guitar and played with several different bands until forming a group called The Mojos, managed by his dad. The group did pretty well, and in March 1964 they had a Top-10 hit with 'Everything's Alright' and followed up with two further Top-30 singles by the end of that year.

Hit records brought the band several television appearances but around 1967, Lewis decided his pop days were over and took odd jobs including lorry driving to pay the bills. Then, one morning he woke up and decided he wanted to be an actor, even though he had no background in acting, had never even seen a play nor been to a theatre in his life. 'I was that ignorant, but acting was almost a natural progression from pop music for me. Because of the pop scene, I was a bigger actor before I became an actor. You need guts to stand up in front of a screaming audience with only a microphone to hide behind. I went off to drama college and had to work really hard to get up to scratch. Then I came out in 1970 and got my first job.'

A TV part as a retarded Liverpool lad locked away in an attic in the police series *Z Cars*, followed by a blink-and-you'll miss-him movie role playing a bearded rugby player in the bawdy movie romp *Confessions Of A Driving Instructor*, set Lewis on his way. Within five years of leaving drama college, he had found fame on TV in *The Cuckoo Waltz*.

A three-in-a-bedsit comedy for ITV, *The Cuckoo Waltz* won strong enough audiences to warrant 3 series from Granada between 1975 and 1977. The comedy centred around hard-up newly-weds Chris and Fliss and their twin babies, who have to share their sparsely furnished Chorlton-cum-Hardy accommodation with Chris's best friend Gavin when he parts from his wife and is forced to leave the matrimonial home.

While the newly-weds eke out a living, wealthy young air-freight executive Gavin moves his fancy furniture into the bedsit, along with his expensive hi-fi, a well-stocked drinks cabinet and his bulging wardrobe. He flaunts his wealth and generally behaves like a cad. Lewis made the most of the role and might have made a fourth series of *The Cuckoo Waltz* if Brian Clemens had not come calling and snapped him up for *The Professionals*. The role of Bodie could hardly have been more different from Gavin Rumsey, and Lewis jumped at it.

Martin was unable to hide his disappointment that Anthony Andrews had been passed over in favour of Lewis. And Lewis initially did himself no favours on his very first day of filming an episode called 'Old Dog With New Tricks' when his nerves got the better of him. The crew, who had briefly filmed with Andrews, were waiting to see how Lewis would perform in comparison with the now-departed actor. Needless to say, Martin was an extremely interested observer as well, and Lewis knew it.

Lewis's very first scene required him to pull off a tricky manoeuvre with a then little-known actress called Pamela Stephenson. Pamela, now probably better known as Mrs Billy Connolly, played a hospital nurse who was being held hostage by an unbalanced youth threatening to blow her to smithereens in a novel way: he had placed a live grenade in her bra. It fell to Lewis, as Bodie, to rescue Nurse Bolding by tearing open Pamela's top, grabbing the grenade and then hurling it into a bin some 25 feet away.

Lewis was nervous enough anyway, as it was his first day in front of the cameras, but having to plunge a hand into Pamela's cleavage, retrieve the grenade and throw it accurately into the bin didn't make it any easier for him – especially as Andrews had accomplished it in just two takes. 'I took about 7 takes,' said Lewis. 'But I passed the test and carried on in the series.'

If there was noticeable friction and mutual suspicion between Martin and Lewis at first, their relationship thawed when Lewis rapidly began to prove himself in the role of Bodie, and Martin was moved to acknowledge to his co-star that he was doing a good job. Years later, Martin revealed on TV: 'I said to Lew: "Look, you probably know I didn't want you to do this. I was not in favour of it and absolutely fought against it. But I've changed my mind: I think you're really great in the part and can we be friends?" I think he still thought I was an arsehole – for a while.'

Clemens commented: 'I think that Martin resented Anthony Andrews going, because Anthony was an actor of some note and Martin could relate to him. When we brought in Lewis and he hadn't really been acting very long and had been the drummer in the Mojos and so on, I think Martin didn't have respect for him initially. He didn't think he was much of an actor. But of course you can't make a series like that without improving every single day and I think Lewis was perfectly okay and became better and better – but then so did Martin as the series progressed.'

In another surprise casting, the role of George Cowley, Doyle and Bodie's scathing taskmaster of a boss, eventually went to Gordon Jackson. Clive Revill was initially in the frame to play Cowley, but he was unwilling to commit himself until he'd learned whether a pilot show he had made in America was to be turned into a series. Albert Fennell then thought of Jackson, with whom he had previously worked.

An immensely likeable Scot, Jackson was an established character actor with more than 30 years of experience behind him. As befitted his international TV star status, he was to be paid £3,700 an episode. Among his many acting credits, he had not only shone in a substantial part among a starry Hollywood cast in one of the classic wartime movies, *The Great Escape*, but by now he had become recognised around the world for his major role in the beautifully-set ITV saga *Upstairs, Downstairs*.

Jackson and his silver salver eye-catchingly stamped his authority on that show below stairs as the starchy, scrupulously correct butler Hudson in the gaslight drama about the fortunes of an aristocratic Edwardian family and their salt-of the-earth servants, who were living at 165 Eaton Square in posh Belgravia. A series for all ages and all classes about age and class, it ran for 68 episodes and dominated ITV drama for the first half of the 1970s.

Born in 1923 in Glasgow, Jackson had begun acting as a schoolboy and, like Martin, his interest had been sparked through the tutelage of an English teacher who was keen on amateur dramatics. He did a few radio broadcasts in Scotland and when he was 17, he was offered a small part in a wartime propaganda film called *The Foreman Went To France*. At the time, Jackson was an engineering apprentice and he had no intention of becoming an actor for a living. But the offer of another film persuaded him to make a go of it and he was rarely out of work thereafter. 'Character men always get more work than stars,' he used to say, modestly describing himself as 'a jobbing actor, a well-known face, like "Katie" in the Oxo ads – I'm not one for stardom.' An eminently respectable and well-respected man, Jackson didn't drink alcohol and could remember being drunk only once in his life.

When *Upstairs, Downstairs* began in 1971, Jackson had made an immediate impact playing Hudson, as the *Daily Mirror* commented, 'with an air of a man who'd been a preacher in some joyless kirk.' He professed never to have met a butler in his life and said Hudson stood for everything he disliked, but his starchy stiffness was in part due to an accident that almost forced him to forego the role.

On the eve of the first day's filming, he came away from a car crash with broken bones in his hand and had 5 stitches inserted in a cut over one eye. The injuries required him to turn his left profile towards the camera and do everything with his left hand. He was still busy filming one final series of the London Weekend drama when he was picked to play Cowley. And so keen was everyone for Jackson to play the CI5 boss that they agreed to delay the start of filming of *The Professionals* until June 1977, by which time he would have completed his final *Upstairs, Downstairs* commitments.

By a twist of fate, this phenomenally successful series was finally drawing to an end with the arrival of Anthony Andrews, no less, playing the Marquis of Stockbridge, who would provide a happy finale by marrying Lesley-Anne Down's flapper-turned-war-heroine Georgina.

The choice of Jackson to play Cowley was certainly a brave one, very definitely casting against type. He clearly wanted to show he had more in his repertoire than *Upstairs, Downstairs*, but some fans of the series found it hard not to think of him as Hudson. They were shocked to see their favourite TV

Top: Martin Shaw and Jill Allen outside St Pancras Town Hall following their wedding on News Year's Eve 1968.

© *Empics*

Bottom: Martin as hippy Robert Croft with fellow cast members of *Coronation Street*.

© *ITV*

Top: Martin joined Robin Nedwell and George Layton for medical mahem in *Doctor in the House*, 1969.

Bottom: With Pauline Collins in *The Mating Machine*, 1970.

Top and bottom right: In Polanski's *The Tragedy of Macbeth*, one of the high spots of Martin's career. He played Banquo in the Polish director's controversial 1971 movie version of Shakespeare's play.

© *Everett Collection/Rex Features*

Bottom left: Martin as Frank Tully in 1973's *Helen: A Woman of Today*.

© *London Weekend Television/Rex Features*

On set with Cheryl Hall in *The Villains*, which dramatized the lives of criminals both famous and obscure, 1972.

Martin Shaw with distinctive poodle perm as Raymond Doyle in *The Professionals*, the role that made him a TV sex symbol.

© *Chris Capstick/Rex Features*

Raymond Doyle in action.　　　© John Curtis/London Weekend Television/Rex Features

Top: In 1980 at the ITV Awards, *The Professionals* was voted Programme Of The Year. In April 1981, Bodie and Doyle were voted TV's Most Compulsive Male Characters in the *TV Times* Top Ten Awards. Here they are pictured with Gordon Jackson, who played George Cowley.   © *Stills Press Agency/Rex Features*

Bottom: Martin's permed and pouting image went up on countless schoolgirls' bedroom walls, but he later condemned the character of CI5 agent Ray Doyle as a 'violent puppet'.

© *Rex Features*

Top left and bottom: In *The Last Place on Earth*, Martin played Captain Scott, and later said, 'My work there is the hardest thing I have ever done from a physical point of view'.

© *ITV/Rex Features*

Top right: As Jack Butcher in the dramatisation of Dennis Potter's *Cream in my Coffee*, 1980.   © *London Weekend Television/Rex Features* butler in the very first episode of *The Professionals*, 'Private Madness, Public Danger' – threatening to force-feed a drug dealer with dope.

During 'pre-pre-production' meetings, one of the topics under discussion was how the dynamic duo would be dressed for their roles. Taking a lead from James Bond's smooth wardrobe, the producers made it clear that they envisaged Bodie and Doyle wearing suits with their hair cut short. Martin was appalled; he thought they were way wide of the mark. He told them in no uncertain terms that jeans and long hair were in, but the bosses would not be swayed and went so far as to warn him that if he turned up for filming wearing jeans then he would immediately be sent home.

He knew it was a risk, but Martin showed them just what he thought of their directive by turning up with his naturally curly hair in a long shaggy perm, and wearing jeans and a leather jacket. Much to his amusement, the director – who knew nothing of the wardrobe threat – looked him up and down, nodded approvingly and said: 'Yeah, that's nice.'

Knowing there was no way that such an individual style could quickly be altered, Martin had deliberately gone for a perm. The only alternative would have been to shear the whole lot off and the producers were unlikely to take such a drastic step: a bald Doyle was not what they were after. Martin's shaggy curls certainly gave him a very different image, and he saw it as a form of disguise for his otherwise distinctive features. He had hit on the idea of a bubble cut, thanks to his last major job before *The Professionals*, a BBC production of Shakespeare's *Love's Labours Lost* which had been filmed in the grounds of

Glyndebourne Opera House. To counter the awful weather during filming, a make-up girl had given him a perm to stop his long, straight locks from becoming limp and straggly.

When he brought this style to *The Professionals*, Lewis nicknamed him 'the bionic golliwog' – even on screen. In an episode called 'Hiding To Nothing', Bodie demanded to know: 'How come the bionic golly gets all the best bits?'

Martin's bubble perm did not go down well with Clemens. 'Martin settled on a hairstyle which I didn't think was great. I think he thought he was looking too close to Lewis, and yet actually it was sort of an actor's frailty because he didn't look a bit like Lewis.'

Like it or lump it – and female fans of *The Professionals* mostly loved it – the poodle perm was there to stay and was regularly maintained by Keith at trendy Knightsbridge salon Smile for just over £20 a time. Just as Joanna Lumley had launched the special 'Purdey' cut in *The New Avengers* which had become all the rage, Martin's hairstyle also soon became a familiar fashion favoured by many a top footballer of the day, not least England hero Kevin Keegan. He received dozens of letters from both sexes wanting to know where he had his hair done and hairdressers made a fortune from customers who requested the 'Doyle' look.

Prior to filming, Martin and Lewis were subjected to some tough days of intensive training to get them fit for what was aiming to be a fast-moving action-packed series. Martin was far from unfit anyway, thanks to daily exercises, regular games of squash, his horse riding and love of rock climbing. Come filming, however, he was grateful for the strenuous training schedule he and Lewis had undergone. In the action scenes, the camera often stayed on Bodie and Doyle for a long time and, if he was running at full tilt, Martin wanted to appear athletic, not about to run out of breath. 'If you're going to be believable as a couple of high-powered terrorist busters, then it's no good limping round the set like a wounded tortoise,' was the way he put it.

An SAS weapons expert sergeant-major also took the duo out into the country to a secret SAS training establishment to show them a variety of violent tricks from the field of combat and self-defence, including how to kill an adversary with their bare hands. Both Martin and Lewis were disturbed to discover how lethal a man could be with just his hands. The pair were also taught the rudiments of handling explosives.

When it came to Bodie and Doyle's weaponry, neither Martin nor Lewis was unfamiliar with guns. Lewis had been a member of a rifle club for 5 years and was beating police marksmen in competitions when he was only 14. He also owned a sizeable private collection of pistols and firearms. Martin, for his part, had a grandfather who was a gunsmith and both his parents were good shots – 'My mother could clean a fairground out of coconuts... It was a rare occasion indeed for me to be allowed to hold one of my grand father's works of art, because that is what they were,' he once recalled.

The technicalities of stuntwork, and film and stage fighting had of course been a part of Martin's curriculum at the London Academy of Music and Dramatic Art so he already knew about tumbling, how to fall, and how to throw and take a punch. But *The Professionals* required a great deal more abilities and stunt arranger Peter Brayham coached both Martin and Lewis through various other skills. The actors resolved to take on as many of the stunts as Brayham allowed, considering it was all part of their acting craft. They also spent 5 days speeding around a skidpan at a police driving instruction centre to learn how to skid and spin a car.

The pair emerged as better drivers but Gordon Jackson – partly because his eve-of-filming car accident was still fresh in his mind – was a distinctly nervy passenger when either Martin or Lewis was at the wheel. It was the only time during filming when he ever appeared the slightest bit ruffled. 'I didn't enjoy being in a car driven by either of the boys,' he later admitted. 'Both Lewis and Martin are very good drivers but I found it very difficult to remember my lines and appear calm while we were flashing along private country roads at 99 miles an hour.

'The boys drive themselves and we have to switch on the camera in the car and set off. I remember one scene where Martin was driving along and gaily overtaking other stunt cars. I was trying to say my lines and keep my nerve while keeping one eye on the road. I was thinking: "Are we going to make it?"' The cars used in the series included the Triumph TR7, Ford Escort and Ford Capri, the last of which became synonymous with *The Professionals*. All of them took a hammering, often driven to the limit of their revs in second gear as the stunts dictated.

It didn't take a genius to work out from the start that exciting physical action was the name of the game rather than strong emotional characterisation. The dialogue was never going to be the obvious strongpoint of *The Professionals*, but when either Martin or Lewis moaned about the quality of their lines, Peter Brayham, the chief stunt arranger, had the perfect answer: 'You tell me when a show is advertised as being "dialogue-packed" and that's when I'm out of business!' he would say.

However, 6 weeks into filming of the first series, Martin dropped a bombshell: he wanted out. Even in those few short weeks he had become desperately dissatisfied with the direction the show was taking as well as the acting limitations of his part in it. Martin felt he had created Ray Doyle in the very first episode of *The Professionals,* but then rapidly realised there was nowhere else for the character to go. He later explained: 'Without, I hope, sounding too pretentious, an actor is not a puppet. An actor is someone who creates and it's very difficult to try to create when you've got somebody's fist down your throat and your arm up your back.'

Disillusioned and fed up, he sat down and wrote a letter of resignation. 'I said: "I'm unhappy, this isn't working, it's not me and you will let me go, won't you?"' He believed that as he no longer wished to work on *The Professionals* there would be no problem and he would be released from his contract.

But he could not have been more wrong. His resignation was rejected out of hand. 'They said: "Are you out of your mind?" I'd thought that if a person was unwilling to work, you couldn't, as this was an artistic endeavour, force them to do so – which, of course, they could, they were entitled to, and they did.'

The LWT bosses were shocked by Martin's request to be released. In fact, Brian Clemens had always envisaged CI5 as an organisation where new personnel could join and so it would not have been difficult to replace Martin by bringing in a new CI5 operative. But he had a 4-year contract, they were only 6 weeks into filming and LWT were pleased with what was already in the can, so Martin's request was rejected outright. Some 3 years later in 1980, in an episode in Series Four called 'Involvement', either by accident or design Doyle was seen slamming his revolver down on Cowley's desk and offering to resign. 'You can't!' Cowley barked back at him. The irony of the scene was not lost on the other cast members and crew.

Clemens was not altogether totally surprised at Martin's stance. He'd seen it happen before – actors would achieve success on TV but at the same time find resentment, and probably no little envy, among their art-for-art's-sake peers who would admonish them for 'doing that television crap' while they themselves might be earnestly carrying a spear at some minor theatre.

Martin now had to accept that he was locked into *The Professionals* for 4 long years. Worse, it became apparent that because the demanding shooting schedule ate up the majority of the year, there would be no time for him to appear in anything else, and fewer and fewer chances to spend time with Jill and their young family. There was nothing he could do but get on with it.

'Private Madness, Public Danger', the first episode of *The Professionals* went out on ITV on 30 December 1977, and was predictably savaged by the majority of the critics, notably by the well-respected Philip Purser, who said, 'Of all the rotten new breed of thuggish cops and secret agents, this little gang is the least attractive… The curly-headed one reminds me fatally of Harpo Marx.'

But Clemens could point to ratings that were extremely encouraging for LWT and soon the show became a massive hit as the public warmed to Bodie and Doyle in their tight flared jeans. Just as he had hoped, female viewers found the two stars sexily attractive, and male viewers liked the duo's macho dynamism. For its time, the show was fast-paced and featured plenty of action-packed sequences with the necessary screeching of tyres, shoot-outs, explosions, burning buildings and the like. And, just as Clemens had also hoped, *The Professionals* proved to have international appeal. It was eventually sold to more than 50 different countries around the world, thereby making Martin a truly international star. Viewers in Libya were so convinced that CI5 actually existed that they besieged the British Embassy in Tripoli after the People's Bureau shooting drama in London with shouts of 'Down with CI5!'

Within weeks of its launch in the UK, the fan mail started to pour in for Martin and Lewis, prompting the formation of a fan club. The tabloids quickly picked up on TV's newest 'superheroes' and Martin and Lewis were touted as the sexiest stars on TV. The *Sun* newspaper, famous for its topless Page Three girls, even appeased its female readers by printing a picture of a bare-chested moustachioed Martin, looking suitably hunky, as their 'Page Seven Fella'. Later the tabloid used another photograph of Martin to present him to their readers as their 'Daily Male'.

The rapidly growing popularity of the programme meant

that he was becoming increasingly recognised wherever he went and he found it a constant irritation. On the rare occasions when he went into a pub, there was always the danger that someone who'd had too much to drink would see him as a challenge and would want to find out just how tough he really was. The attention was ceaseless, and there was nowhere to hide. Strangers stopped and stared at him, others pointed him out in the street or pestered him for autographs, often at inopportune moments. Martin was staggered when he was once asked for his autograph by a fan who had somehow spotted him while he was on his motorbike wearing a full-faced crash helmet and balaclava.

Some autograph hunters he found downright rude – he was livid to be hassled on one occasion when on a visit with his children to the Science Museum in London. Those who gave him unwelcome attention could get short shrift. Strangers who came up to him intrusively and said, as per usual: 'It's you, isn't it?' might get the flippant answer: 'Yes, that's right, all day it's been me, and yesterday and tomorrow.' One fan even complained to London Weekend that when he asked Martin for an autograph for his daughter, Martin allegedly replied: 'That's a fair swap.'

'I like fame when it's appropriate, when it's inappropriate it's detestable,' he once explained on Radio 4's *Midweek* programme. As for being asked for autographs: 'I used to beat myself up five minutes after being very brusque or even rude to somebody. I'd think: "Oh God, why did I do that? What an awful person I am." These people are paying my wages.'

In another radio interview, this time with Radio 1's Andy

Peebles, Martin conceded: 'I asked for the recognition by virtue of the fact that I did *The Professionals* and got all this fame. Somewhere along the line I must have wanted it. Very often I find it intensely irritating. I've got to learn to be graceful about it. Usually what I find is that there is a fair amount of aggression about the approaches I get which is more to do with jealousy, I think, than it has to do with wanting to challenge me.'

But he hated all the attention and the growing perception of him as a glamorous action man. As a rounded, versatile actor, he loathed the way the press constantly described him as 'TV tough guy Martin Shaw'. It irked him intensely, and he wasn't afraid of saying so. No one who knew Martin well doubted his sincerity. But to those outside of the acting world and to the casual observer, his stance made him appear ungrateful for the chance he had been given in *The Professionals*. He was on his way to becoming an international TV star and, in a profession where so many were out of work, there were plenty of his peers who would gladly have swapped places with him.

And yet his irritation was wholly understandable. Up until *The Professionals* he'd had a flourishing career as a chameleon-like actor that had enabled him to move smoothly from role to very different role on stage, in TV and in movies. He'd spent 15 years as an actor before Ray Doyle had come along and in that time no one had been able to pin a label upon him. 'I play hundreds of people and my career doesn't begin and end with Ray Doyle,' he said, desperate to get himself back on a firm artistic footing.

As with many other internationally popular television series,

The Professionals was backed up both in the UK and overseas with a wide range of marketing tie-ins exploiting the characters in the programme, which just served to raise his profile even higher. Martin complied with the marketing demands under some sufferance. There were no less than 8 editions of *The Professionals Annuals* published between 1978 and 1984, and a further 15 paperback novelisations of the stories, which were specially written for the show. In addition, several official *Professionals* magazines were published as well as poster magazines with pictures of Martin and Lewis looking mean and tough on their front covers.

There was even a *Professionals* 'Crimebuster Kit', aimed at kids between the ages of 5 and 11, comprising a toy pistol with removable silencer and telescopic sight, a magazine for the gun plus a shoulder holster, a secret radio transmitter, a code watch and identification cards. On the box was a picture of Martin, wearing a suitably pained expression, holding the pistol and Lewis lending an ear to the transmitter. Two years later came a Corgi gift car set comprising a silver-grey Capri and plastic figurines of Bodie, Doyle and Cowley. When the show was at its peak, the merchandise flew off the toy-shop shelves.

Not satisfied with just pinning a poster of him on their bedroom wall, Martin's more devoted fans could also buy a full-colour, 250-piece jigsaw puzzle picture of their idol with a gun tucked under one arm. It says much for the faith of the marketing men in their ability to shift thousands of Martin Shaw jigsaws that at great expense they hired Lord Lichfield, photographer cousin of the Queen, to take Martin's picture.

Though Martin accepted that a degree of promotion for *The*

Professionals was part of the job, back in the days when he was working alongside Laurence Olivier, becoming a pin-up poster boy and a jigsaw puzzle was surely not part of his plan.

Such was the impact of the show that the more gullible members of the public absurdly expected Lewis and Martin to hang out together more or less twenty-four hours a day. Lewis got annoyed when people who spotted him out and about stupidly asked: 'Where's the other one?' 'Martin and I are not Siamese twins, you know,' he'd snap. 'We lead quite separate lives off the set, but people always expect us to travel in pairs.'

Whenever the two men made public appearances they were met by screaming girls. Some fainted with excitement, others tried to tear bits of clothing off them and the hysteria was likened to Beatlemania. Martin was nearly strangled when one such appearance got out of hand. Two women got hold of his scarf, tugged the ends in different directions and wouldn't let go!

A teen magazine voted him as the sexiest man on TV and the fan letters from females became progressively saucier, many sending photographs in various states of undress, enclosing their telephone number and address, and suggesting a suitable time for him to call. Luckily, Martin was balanced enough to know that the fans were not really in love with him but instead with an image on a TV screen. However, his uncourted fan worship took an altogether sinister turn when an obsessed fan found out where he lived and forged his signature on a Post Office form in order to have his mail redirected to her home. The woman fraudulently signed an interception order at the Post Office and paid for all Martin's post, including bank statements, acting contracts and his personal letters, to be sent to her own address. For one whole year his mail was delivered to her and she would open the letters, read them, then reseal the envelopes before hand-delivering them to his address the following day. If there was any post she felt he should not have, she did not deliver it at all.

It was only when he complained to the Post Office that a parcel he had received had been tampered with that Martin discovered what had been going on. An investigation uncovered the awful truth and later a court ordered the woman not to harass Martin. From then on, the Royal Mail tightened its security. 'It was ghastly, like being burgled every day,' said Martin, and he knew why it had happened: 'The fame was to blame.'

He was confused and appalled by the stardom that had been thrust upon him by *The Professionals*. Unlike many other actors to whom stardom was a happy by-product of success, Martin found it unpleasant. The frenzied adulation, the seeking of favours, the publicity and the constant scrutiny of all things Martin Shaw were factors he hadn't anticipated. This unpleasant side-effect of his fame was another contributing factor towards his declared wish to quit *The Professionals*. The pressures of his commitments to the series also contributed to his split with Jill Allen.

There was never any suggestion – or complaint from the production team – that Martin wasn't giving his all to the role of Doyle once he had made it known that he was desperate to leave the show. He realised he had made a mistake in signing up as Doyle for 4 years, but he also knew it was his duty to fulfil his contract once permission to leave had been refused. He had simply had no idea that *The Professionals* would be such a huge success and now he had no option other than to go along with it.

By the end of the first series, *The Professionals* was winning a healthy audience of around 10 million and the commissioning of that second series by LWT was a mere formality. The production moved out of Pinewood to the Lee International studios at Wembley and, because as much as 90 per cent of the series was to be shot on location, it allowed easier access to film with grittier London backdrops.

It took around 10 days to film each episode, and it was not uncommon for Martin and Lewis to work 16-hour days, a pace which inevitably took its toll both mentally and physically, and finally on Martin's family life. After 14 years of marriage to Jill, in early 1982 he moved out of the family home and into a London flat, both of them taking care to make the split as amicable as possible for the sake of their three children. The separation made him treasure his time away from *The Professionals* even more, so that he could maintain regular and loving contact with his kids. He remained friends with Jill and was a regular Sunday visitor to see Sophie, Luke and Joe, and take them out for the day.

Although *The Professionals* took him away a great deal, he and Jill had begun to grow apart anyway. They had married very young when they were not long out of drama school and in the intervening years they had both changed. 'He and mum were always friends,' Martin's daughter Sophie was quoted as saying very recently: 'If it doesn't sound too odd, they are a great example of how to split up well. If only we could all behave as well and handle things as impressively as they have.' Joe Shaw, her brother, agrees: 'Even after the separation, I never saw Mum and Dad argue.'

In November 1978, when the second series was already going out on ITV and continuing to grow in popularity, Martin ruffled a few feathers by revealing in an interview with top TV writer Margaret Forwood of the *Sun* that he was still anxious to leave the show. 'If I could leave tomorrow, I would,' he told her, stressing that he was not criticising the show, merely the constrictions placed upon him as an actor and that, if permitted, he would leave with great respect for all the people involved with the show, 'and with heartfelt thanks for all their understanding.'

He went on to state that he felt imprisoned, explaining his predicament thus: 'A prisoner in Wormwood Scrubs doing four years knows that he is going to get out at the end of so many years, but while he is there, he doesn't like it.' But he added: 'If I'm held to my contract I shall go back and do it to the very best of my ability. I shall dedicate myself to it as hard as I can, because that's the only way I know how to work.'

Ironically, soon afterwards, filming of *The Professionals* came to an unexpected and embarrassing halt that November when Lewis Collins broke an ankle. The actor had long been a keen parachutist and had trained with the Territorial Army Airborne Division. He had performed around 300 free falls and on 4 occasions he had had to use his reserve 'chute when the main one failed to open.

Now, having emerged relatively unscathed from various

carefully controlled explosions, orchestrated punch-ups and car crashes for the cameras, Lewis unfortunately broke his ankle while performing yet another parachute jump with some friends during a weekend off. For the production team it was the worst possible news. There were already 10 episodes safely in the can, but there was no way Lewis could complete filming of the remaining 3 until his ankle had healed.

Again, just as he had done when Martin had asked to leave, Clemens considered re-writing the scripts to include drafting in a new CI5 character to fill the gap while Bodie was seen recovering with his leg in plaster or possibly even in a wheelchair. It would have been perfectly feasible for him to have sustained a bad injury while in CI5 service, but in the end it was decided that it would be best just to suspend production for 3 months and begin filming again in March the following year.

A mighty wrath descended upon Lewis for halting production in this manner. Under the terms of their contracts, neither Martin nor Lewis were permitted to take part in any sports or activities off-set which might incur any sort of film-stopping injury. Much to Martin's regret, this also included horse riding and rock climbing, two of his favourite pursuits. Though he liked nothing better than setting off for Snowdonia to go climbing with his friend Mike, he could understand the concerns of his employers. With climbing, there was always more than a hint of danger, and in one interview Martin admitted: 'I've never done it without feeling frightened – I don't know why I want to do it, perhaps the reward is communicating with nature. There's a feeling of confidence between you and the rock.'

By this time he was an accomplished climber with some 7 years' experience behind him, including regular climbs at Llanberis Pass in north Wales. The longest climb he had ever made lasted more than 2 hours and in his 7 years of climbing he had never had an accident, but even the best can make mistakes. On one particular climb in Wales he made an error that could have been fatal. Martin had embarked on a climb that appeared to hold few terrors and reached a broad ledge that was about 8 feet wide. His first task should have been to secure himself to the rock face while his climbing partner Mike came up on the rope that he was holding; but for once, he forgot to perform the safety procedure, which soon placed them both in grave danger.

'I just sat there on the ledge with nothing to prevent me from falling,' he recounted. 'Suddenly Mike shouted: "I'm going to have to go down a bit." Then he let go of the rock face so I could ease him down on the rope. Of course, I wasn't secured and I started to slide forward. I realised I'd made a terrible blunder; I hung on to the rope with Mike swinging on the end. As I slipped forward, my legs went over the edge and the rest of me was about to follow.'

Martin leant back as he desperately strained to hold on to the rope, literally for dear life. However, that meant he couldn't see Mike below him and therefore couldn't tell how far his pal was above the narrow ledge that he was aiming for: just two feet and he could safely let go, but ten feet and Mike could land awkwardly and break a leg.

Now Martin had to make an agonising decision extremely quickly. If he didn't let go, he was in danger of being pulled clean off the ledge, plummeting hundreds of feet to almost certain death, and the likelihood was that he would take Mike to his doom with him. His heart was in his mouth as he let go. 'I was mortified,' he recalled, 'but eventually called out: "Mike are you all right?" Then I explained what happened and he said calmly: "I thought the last two feet were a bit bumpy."' Fortunately for them both, the drop had been just that: a couple of feet.

The injury to Lewis Collins and the shutting down of the production may have afforded Martin a welcome few weeks away from the rigours of filming, but when production resumed again in the spring of 1979, it was announced the intention was to film the outstanding 3 episodes from Series Two and then follow on immediately with a third series, making a total of 18 episodes back-to-back, stretched over a period of 8 months.

It would be a test of stamina for everyone involved, and Martin resolved to try and get into peak condition before the cameras started rolling – but that was far from easy when his contract restricted him from participating in any activity that could possible be called dangerous. Eventually both Martin and Lewis raised their fitness levels to new heights when they were seconded into the RAF for a few days and put under the command of a tough, no-nonsense parachute-training instructor who put them through their paces. They had to get up early and report for strenuous workouts at a nearby naval base. There was one consolation, however – the base was regularly used as a training establishment for Wrens.

By now, Martin and Lewis had developed a healthy respect

for each other – and a shared sense of frustration that they weren't able to make more of their characters. They were very different men, but they shared a sense of humour and got through the tough times by playing jokes on each other. Although they rarely socialised away from filming they would meet up occasionally to make music, jam together and put a few tunes down on tape. Martin liked to play guitar and piano, and he bought himself an expensive synthesiser that gave him great pleasure. When *The Professionals* was the hottest show on TV, he was sounded out about making a record and eventually released 'Cross My Heart And Hope To Die' in 1984.

During filming the two enjoyed the camaraderie, but they wouldn't have been human if they hadn't had their disagreements and there were some explosive spats while working in such close proximity under extreme pressure for long periods of time. Martin likened it to living in a pressure cooker with the lid firmly jammed on. Never in his life had he expended so much physical and mental energy, especially when shooting consecutive episodes, which of necessity required a mental change of gear. 'If you put 2 people together every day 14 hours a day with the stresses and tensions, then there will be explosions,' he said. 'There were one or two arguments, but nothing that wasn't resolved. The best thing about that relationship was that we knew how to work with each other and we had a very good sense of humour about the whole thing.'

Martin went further than that when interviewed for Channel 4's *Within These Walls*. He said: 'I think if you were doing a film, and you wanted… in the short term, you needed, a sparky abrasive relationship, then it might just be a good idea to put two people together for six months and see what happens. But if you were intending to put people together for four years, it was stupid.'

On one particularly bad day when things had gone anything but smoothly, both men were thoroughly fraught and wound up, and Martin took exception to something Lewis had said. As was his wont, Martin shrugged and walked away – he had very rarely lost his temper in his life. But for once he was absolutely seething, and he turned around to confront his co-star and found himself saying that if Lewis ever said anything like it again, then he would kill him. 'I heard the words coming out,' he later recounted, 'but it didn't feel as though it was me saying them. He backed off, there was a silence and nothing else that we could say to each other. Afterwards I felt ashamed – not only was it a stupid thing to say, I'd thought my self-control was better than that.'

A year later, it was Lewis's turn to explode with anger after Martin had made a few choice remarks. He went mad, Martin remembered. 'I was terrified because he's built like a brick outhouse and I thought he was going to kill me. By that time I'd realised more about my honesty and I told him later: "I want you to know that when you were angry I was really frightened." It brought us much closer together. But it shows what can happen when you're working at a frantic pace.' Fortunately, the two stars never came to blows. Martin liked to have a boxer's punchball in his dressing room, and whenever frustration got the better of him he could take a swing at that.

For 12 to 15 hours a day, 5 days a week, Martin and Lewis worked flat out, acrobatically hurling themselves around.

Master stunt arranger Peter Brayham encouraged the actors to perform as many of their own stunts as possible, using stuntmen only when the stars might be in serious danger. Gone were the days when film stars could turn up on set somewhat the worse for drink and let their double stand in for them on the action scenes. The drive now was for reality and that meant the two of them stepping up to the mark.

Martin learned to snatch every moment of sleep he possibly could, even if it meant just closing his eyes for ten minutes in the back of a car. A driver would pick him up at 6.15 in the mornings and deliver him home late in the evening when he would soak himself in a bath while listening to some Bach and try to gather his thoughts for the next day's filming. The long hours meant little time for a social life and he strived to maintain his fitness to get through the series in one piece, once a week making a visit to an osteopath. He supplemented his vegetarian diet by drinking black tea with honey for extra energy and had the same lunch every day – a large salad with jacket potato – thereby avoiding anything fattening. He told friends he now knew why Hollywood stars were pampered so much – it was to keep them alive and fresh for the next scene.

In such an action-packed series it was inevitable that Martin would collect his fair share of knocks and bruises, only twice was he seriously hurt and once when he suffered concussion after a bad fall. He was supposed to use his shoulder to break his fall on to a mattress but he misjudged it and instead his head impacted with the concrete floor. For an anxious few moments for everyone, Martin was completely unconscious and was immediately rushed off to hospital. When he came round he couldn't see or hear anything properly but, as his head cleared, he insisted he was fine and ready to get back to work. However, the medical staff wisely kept him in the hospital for 6 hours while they carried out some tests to assess if he had suffered any real damage to his head. On learning that they planned to keep him in hospital under observation for 24 hours, he elected to sign himself out and go back to the film set. In the best show business traditions, the show had to go on.

He was also in the wars during a scene filmed at White Waltham airfield. In the course of being slammed hard up against a hangar door, a bolt on the door dug into the base of his spine causing the right side of his hip to go into spasm. Once again he chose to shrug it off so as not to disrupt filming. On another occasion, he was knocked out again when he hit his head on a bridge while pretending to leap for cover in a shoot-out. And in yet another scene where he had his hands tied behind his back, Lewis contrived to cut Martin's little finger with a knife instead of the cords that bound him. When the director saw the blood was starting to flow, he asked Martin if he was happy to continue filming the scene as he felt it was going so well. Only when the scene was safely in the can was a doctor called in to staunch the flow and stitch the wound.

Perhaps the most hazardous moment for Martin came when he was required to run from an exploding car in an episode in Series Two called 'Hunter, Hunted'. The plot had him driving away from a girlfriend's flat and discovering his brakes and steering had been tampered with. It then called for him to bring the car to a halt and leap out seconds before it exploded. The scene was set up with the utmost care by Peter Brayham and timed to perfection so that both Martin's feet were in the air when the blast hit him. Brayham's cue to press the button for the explosion was the split second Martin jumped and crouched at the same time so that the blast would go over and under him, not blow him head over heels. It was expertly done and made for a spectacular stunt. Martin said that the only real danger had been when he was required to stand right up next to the car. It was packed with high explosives and a petrol bomb, and any short circuit in the wiring would have blown him to bits.

Not to be outdone, Lewis Collins can recall a moment of very real alarm when Martin was driving a motorboat and he was leaning to one side, supposedly shooting at some villains they were chasing up the river Thames. When they whizzed round a corner, Lewis lost his balance and toppled overboard. Worryingly, one of his feet had got caught under a seat and he was dragged along for some distance at a speed of 45 knots with his head and torso under the water.

Martin was looking the other way and so was unaware of what was happening. The film crew on another boat screamed at him and frantically gesticulated for him to stop but he thought they were just waving at him and carried on. 'It was only about 30 seconds, but I thought I was finished,' said Lewis. 'When I got out, I said to Martin: "Listen, mate, it's the last episode but I'd like to come out of it alive!"'

By the end of the gruelling 8-month shoot, Martin was at the very end of his tether, experiencing mental and physical exhaustion. After a heavy day's filming, he could become bad-tempered if he was stuck in traffic or if someone or something was irritating him. He was so totally stressed out that he found himself losing all sense of time and continually bursting into tears. 'Physical and mental stress combined with resentment, produces illness,' he said.

Four days after they had completed this lengthiest of film shoots, Lewis telephoned Martin to find out how he was bearing up. After ten minutes of stilted conversation, he admitted that he too had been 'out of his tree' from all their exertions. While sympathising with Lewis, it was a comfort of sorts for Martin to know that his on-screen partner was feeling as strung out as he was. To return his mind and body to normality, Martin had to allow himself to spend the next 5 weeks sleeping and resting as much as he could before heading out of London to spend a few days of quiet recuperation with friends in the country.

The colossal demands placed upon Martin and Lewis during filming were not lost on Gordon Jackson. Clemens described Gordon as the 'oil in the works man' for the way the veteran actor kept everything going smoothly and the set happy. Gordon was always on time, always knew his lines, was always rehearsed and used his experience and maturity to overcome any problems. But he looked on in some amazement as his two young co-stars gave their all and more. 'It's so tiring for them,' he said. 'I have a few days off but they are there all the time; they work non-stop.'

Although Martin's contract did not specifically insist that he take on no other acting work, the filming schedule for *The*

Professionals made it almost impossible for him to seriously consider anything else. He simply had no time to fit in other projects and, during a break in filming in the third series, Gordon Jackson confided to one of the authors that he had some sympathy for him in his struggle to shake off what he perceived to be the artistic straitjacket of *The Professionals*. He could also understand why, as an actor anxious to go on and play a wide range of parts, Martin was concerned about becoming so heavily identified with Ray Doyle.

By now in his mid-fifties, Gordon had 35 years of roles including 50 films behind him, but he readily acknowledged that most people he met instantly thought of him as Hudson in *Upstairs, Downstairs*. To all of America, and in many other countries around the world besides, he was the epitome of the English butler and always would be. When a show was as universally successful as *Upstairs, Downstairs*, typecasting was inevitable and he could see why Martin was kicking against his image as a 'telly tough guy,' as the tabloids liked to call him.

He said of his co-star: ' I can see where he's coming from. He's had good supporting roles in films – he was Banquo in Polanski's *Macbeth*, he's done very good work in the theatre, he's had a wide range of roles on TV, and he's LAMDA-trained. I just don't think he ever dreamed that this show would be so popular as to turn him into a sex symbol, or that he'd find himself featured holding a gun on the front of a *Professionals* box of toys or as a *Professionals* jigsaw puzzle. The press have labelled him a TV tough guy, and I'm sure that isn't how Martin saw his career progressing.

'Martin's shown me, and everyone else, that he's a fine actor.

He's very good as Doyle, and he's been very impressive in several other things I've seen him in. He's a dedicated actor and, as such, he wants to stretch himself and do different things. It may take time for him to move on from his image in *The Professionals*, but I'm confident he will. He's still young and his best days are almost certainly still ahead of him. He will grow as an actor as he gets older.'

For Martin and Lewis, Gordon's quiet professionalism and his vast experience was a calming influence on the set. He just got on with the job, never complained once and was grateful for the chance to show in another high profile series that he could be more than just an ever-so-correct butler.

In the Channel 4 programme *Within These Walls*, shown on 9 April 1996, Martin gave Gordon a glowing tribute. 'Gordon was one of the most delightful, well-balanced and kindest people I've ever met in my life,' he said. 'He had none of these pressures or strains. And he'd say: "Och, dear boy, dinna worry aboot the line – it disnae matter, just say it, say it, say it." And that's what he did!'

Lewis was equally full of praise: 'Cowley was the big bad boss, which was hard for Gordon,' he said. 'I think it was possibly his most testing role because he was such a sweet man. His portrayal had a kind of warmth behind the eyes, even though he was being tough.'

By the time the third series of *The Professionals* hit the screen in November 1979, the show was pulling in a staggering 18 million viewers and was even beating supersoap *Dallas* in the ratings. But Martin was no happier. That same month he outspokenly told Kit Miller, one of Fleet Street's most colourful writers: 'I'd dearly love to pack it in right now.' Miller also famously quoted Martin as saying: 'I'm desperate to become an actor again – all I am now is a violent puppet.'

From day one, the violent content in *The Professionals* was something that had caused controversy. Over the course of its 5-year run, the series pushed boundaries on TV to the limit and constantly had to contend with the anti-violence lobby. 'Clean-up TV' campaigner Mrs Mary Whitehouse of the Viewers and Listeners' Association lambasted the show as 'violent, uncouth and thoroughly unsavoury.' As a peace-loving vegetarian, Martin was frequently quizzed in interviews as to how he managed to balance his own gentle nature with the violence on-screen. There was no conflict, he was just playing games, he said, and doubted whether anyone was likely to have their morals perverted unless they were very easily swayed.

He argued that if the TV companies were creating hard-hitting series like *The Professionals* then the characters should be portrayed as realistically as possible. For too long, TV and the movies had perpetrated lies about the effects of violence and firearms, he said, and pointed out that when he saw his kids playing out games like *The Professionals*, they had no concept that a weapon like the Browning Hi-Power could lift a man into the air and slam him back with a hole in him. 'Unfortunately violence exists and we should be realistic about depicting it,' he reasoned. Part of the fun of *The Professionals*, he felt, was seeing Bodie and Doyle being able to go out and do their work regardless of the rules. But it had to be remembered that CI5 was an amoral organisation.

Brian Clemens preferred to regard the contentious sequences

as action rather than violence. 'We portray things realistically,' he argued, 'otherwise you're left with the now absurd *Starsky And Hutch* situation where they have to play everything with kid gloves and are not even allowed to frisk subjects because that's supposed to be demeaning and look undignified.'

He had a point. Once *The Professionals* had been sold to the Americans, things changed. 'The Americans had these extraordinary rules in force which they [the producers] put in for later series,' Martin revealed when discussing the programme on ITV's *This Morning* in 1997. 'So, if anybody died, they weren't allowed to die with their eyes open. If you smashed somebody in the face that was all right as long as they didn't bleed.'

From the second series onwards, both Martin and Lewis felt that their own ideas as to how their characters and the show could develop were largely ignored. But once the action-packed formula had proved so successful, it was hard for the storywriters to change tack. Script editor Gerry O'Hara convincingly outlined the dilemma in *Primetime* magazine in 1981. 'What I thought I could do as a story editor was bring more depth of character into the stories,' he said. 'I found I couldn't do it so much with the regular characters – more with Cowley than with Bodie and Doyle.

'Bodie and Doyle had degrees of depth – but the secret of these two characters is that the audience sees them differently, sees them as they want to see them. Regrettably, perhaps, on paper they haven't been allowed to get the depth that Martin Shaw and Lewis Collins would have wanted, but they were pipped by their own popularity.

'I'm convinced that the audience sees them in special ways. Little girls see them as the fellas they long to have for themselves; young boys in another way, as the heroes they want to be; mothers and fathers see them as sons they would like to have. Now that sounds absurd because they whip out guns and shoot people to pieces – but I think they're "turn-ons," they're adrenalin releasers for all the different kinds of people in the audience.'

Producer Ray Menmuir put it more forcefully. 'Martin and Lewis used to say: "We want more character." With due respect, what they meant was they wanted more scenes where they could... act with a capital A.'

However, if lack of opportunity led to continual artistic frustration for the show's two young stars, one thing was certain: the viewers were not too bothered, and there was a clutch of awards to show for it. In 1980 at the ITV Awards, *The Professionals* was voted Programme Of The Year. 'We've been very fortunate because we've had the most magnificent crew,' said Martin in acceptance. 'Thank you for your patience and tolerance.' In April of the following year, Bodie and Doyle were voted TV's Most Compulsive Male Characters in the *TV Times* Top Ten Awards. In the same month, *The Professionals* won the ITV Programme Of The Year Award given by the Television and Radio Industries Club.

Despite the constrictions of his contract for *The Professionals*, Martin did manage to go 'over the wall,' as he put it, on a couple of occasions. In 1980 he found the time to fit in a plum TV role playing a 1930s crooner called Jack Butcher in *Cream In My Coffee*, a play by Dennis Potter. The play was screened on

ITV following straight on from an episode of *The Professionals* – fortunate juxtaposition in the schedules that allowed him to demonstrate his range as an actor.

With slicked-back dark hair and moustache, wearing a snazzy striped jacket, a cravat and white flannels, he was almost unrecognisable as the singer with a hotel band. In a classy production, Dame Peggy Ashcroft and Lionel Jeffries played Jean and Bernard Wilsher, an elderly couple who go back to a south-coast hotel to relive memories of staying there 40 years previously when they were young lovers yet to be married. In the story, told in flashback, it transpired that Jean had briefly fallen for the charms of Jack Butcher after her beau had suddenly been called away by a relative who had discovered their secret tryst.

Cream In My Coffee was well received and went on to win a Prix Italia award, Italy's prestigious international prize for outstanding television. For Martin, Jack Butcher was a welcome change from Ray Doyle. In 1981 he also found time to take over, for a short season, the leading role in the West End stage musical *They're Playing Our Song* that co-starred Gemma Craven.

Martin hadn't made it easy for himself, in that he was taking over the song-and-dance role from established actor Tom Conti who had proved a big draw. However, playing Vernon Gersch, an insecure but talented Jewish-American songwriter who falls in love with his scatty female lyricist, was so very different from Ray Doyle that he decided to take it on. He acquitted himself well in what was essentially a two-hander with Gemma, who was eventually succeeded by Sheila Brand. Inevitably, many of the seats at the theatre were filled with female fans of *The Professionals* eager for a glimpse of their TV favourite in the flesh. But the management weren't complaining. It kept the box office ticking over at an unprecedented rate.

Martin was unhappy when flashbulbs went off while he was on stage. 'It is like pulling the plug out in the bath,' he complained to the *Daily Mail*. 'It just drains the energy totally. A play rides on its own energy. It is absolutely like a bubble that is held up by the pressure of the air inside it. There is a balance between the air outside and the air inside and if you introduce a foreign body into it then it goes pop… bang, like that.'

During its run from 1977 to 1983, *The Professionals* successfully staved off competition from an avalanche of cop/detective shows including *Charlie's Angels*, *Hazell*, *Shoestring*, *Target*, *Return Of The Saint*, *The Chinese Detective*, *Bergerac*, *Hart To Hart*, *Hill Street Blues* and *The Gentle Touch*, but as production costs rose, and the cost of hiring equipment such as helicopters became ever more expensive, the show eventually had to come to an end.

In 1981 the news broke that *The Professionals* was finishing and London Weekend Television's switchboard was swamped with calls from angry fans believing they had seen the last of Bodie and Doyle. But they had misinterpreted the story. Yes, *The Professionals* was bowing out, but there would, in fact, be another 11 episodes due for screening towards the end of 1982 and the start of the following year. The final episode was eventually screened on 6 February 1983 and finished with an explosive collision between an inflatable dinghy carrying Bodie and Doyle and the motorboat they were chasing.

Soon after his 4-year servitude was over and the series had finished, Martin was asked on breakfast television whether he hated *The Professionals*. 'No, no no – I don't hate it,' he said. 'There were bits I liked and bits I didn't. But nobody's interested in the bits I liked – they only want to know about the bits I hated. I liked playing with the toys, I liked blowing up cars, I liked playing with machine guns. I liked joking with Lewis Collins, I liked admiring Gordon Jackson's professionalism, I liked earning money, too.'

Something else he liked very much was The Comic Strip's wonderful spoof called *The Bullshitters*. The climax to the show had Bodie and Doyle rolling around on a rubbish tip in their underpants snogging each other. No one laughed louder at this send-up than Martin Shaw. As time moved on, he too was not averse to sending himself up as Ray Doyle. For *Comic Relief* in 1988, millions of viewers saw him in a short sketch entitled 'The Unprofessionals' in which he burst in on three villains and then almost immediately made a sharp exit saying: 'Damn, left my gun on the bus!'

And in 1999, by which time he had stamped his authority as a fine actor on a wide range of roles, he was even able to say: 'It's wonderful that it's become a cult show. I'm not now, nor ever have been, ashamed of playing Doyle, though I wasn't happy about the fame that went with the role. Contrary to some stories, I haven't become "superior" about my work or keen to sweep Doyle under the carpet.'

A great deal has been written about whether Martin did, or did not block repeat screenings of *The Professionals*. At one point there appeared to be a press campaign mounted against him that painted him as a stubborn thespian depriving others in the show of their repeat fees. Much of what was written was nonsense. He merely took a stand because the programme-makers had not renegotiated his contract for repeat showings and understandably he simply wanted a fair fee for the repeats.

To this day *The Professionals* retains a remarkably loyal fan base. Items connected with the show fetch surprisingly high prices on e-bay, and a lively and informative fan site on the internet run by Dave Matthews still receives around 350 hits a day.

Back in 1981, however, after so long away Martin had been grateful to make a return to stage work in *They're Playing Our Song*, and when *The Professionals* finally finished and he was at last free to go after other roles, he described the process of trying to get back to theatre after such a long time away as like trying to get match fit again when some of the muscles have atrophied.

At the time his very real fear was that the producers and directors who remembered him from the broad range of solid work he had done before *The Professionals* had now moved on themselves, and that the new young guns on the block would have their image of him as an actor blurred by the enormous shadow cast by the series. There was now a whole new generation of casting directors, producers and directors too young to have been around when he was doing such good and varied work between 1969 and 1977. He was worried they might form unconscious opinions about him and make judgements on him from what they were seeing in *The Professionals*.

A trip to Australia for a stage role in Simon Gray's *Otherwise Engaged* was a good reminder and helped re-establish his credentials. Next, he was chosen to star in Clifford Odet's play *The Country Girl* as an obnoxious and abrasive, hard-nosed Broadway director from Hell's Kitchen, who becomes involved in backstage dramas.

Set in 1950s New York and Boston, *The Country Girl* was given an out-of-town run at Leatherhead in Surrey before moving into the Apollo, Shaftesbury Avenue, in September 1983. In the pre-London run, a local reviewer decided Martin Shaw was fine on TV, but not up to the serious stage stuff. These comments bothered Martin and he was apprehensive as to how West End audiences would react as opening night neared. But he need not have worried: the reviews were highly complimentary and led to him being reassessed as an actor.

By that time he had bought a remote old crofter's cottage in an isolated area of south-west Scotland that served as an ideal retreat. After the weekend performance of *The Country Girl*, he would leave London at 11.30pm and drive all night to get there, feeling himself becoming more relaxed with every mile he put behind him.

The cottage had a 2-mile approach road followed by a further mile of rough track so that for the last 15 minutes of the drive he could keep it firmly in his sights. He usually managed to arrive by six in the morning and would sleep till noon, then take a re-invigorating walk before spending the evening lazing in front of the fire and driving back to London the next morning. It was just the refreshing break he needed.

In 1982, with *The Professionals* at the peak of its popularity and after his separation from Jill Allen, Martin had quietly got married for a second time to Maggie Mansfield, an ex-nurse who had become an alternative therapist. They managed to wed without a media circus and, with a new wife and new challenges as an actor opening up now *The Professionals* was behind him, Martin had every reason to look forward with confidence.

One of his first steps in getting as far away as possible from Ray Doyle was to take a role as Archibald Carlyle, a 'goody-goody lawyer' in a one-off Victorian melodrama for the BBC called *East Lynne*. The 2-hour play that also starred Jane Asher and Gemma Craven saw Martin's character fall head-over-heels in love and get married, lose his wife over a misunderstanding, get married to someone else, then have his first wife return and have to see his son die! 'But it was still more realistic than the people in *The Professionals*,' he said ruefully.

'Archibald tries to care for people but everything goes wrong,' said Martin. 'But the wonderful thing is that he sticks to his integrity. What's really attractive about him for me is that I've been playing heavy, violent people and it's nice to explore the softer side of my nature.'

He certainly went for variety. He guested on *The Kenny Everett Television Show* and found himself handcuffed to the irrepressible host in what was described as 'the pervert on the train sketch'. And later he went on to star in a futuristic musical called *Facelift* that was set in the year 2074 in which he played a colourful magician called Zax. Describing the role, he said, 'I sing, perform tricks, and saw a woman in half – it's enormous fun.'

Martin even entered the territory of an even more famous Doyle – Sir Arthur Conan Doyle no less – in a US film version of the classic *The Hound of the Baskervilles* in which he played Sir Henry Baskerville. 'He's a nice guy,' he noted. 'He seems open-minded and pleasant and kind, not a negative character at all. I hadn't any previous connection with Sir Arthur Conan Doyle, apart from reading the stories as a kid. The American accent is a bit difficult to sustain because it's not a city accent. It's half-Texan and half-Western.' He welcomed the challenge to get even further away from *The Professionals*. 'The greatest benefit of my career has been the opportunity to play as many different roles as possible,' he said. 'I want to use the widest variety of my ability as possible. As an actor you get a chance to use all sorts of emotions and that must be good.'

CAPTAIN SCOTT

*'I may not have proved a great explorer but we have done the
greatest march ever made and come very near to great success'*
Captain Robert Falcon Scott on his race with
Amundsen to the South Pole

Late in the afternoon of 16 January 1912, Captain Robert
Falcon Scott and his intrepid team of explorers reached
the South Pole, only to find a Norwegian flag that had already
been planted there some 21 days earlier by Scott's great rival,
Roald Amundsen. This shattering moment remains one of the
most poignant in British history and in 1984 it was to provide
Martin Shaw with one of his most physically challenging roles,
playing Scott in *The Last Place On Earth*.

The epic race between the two explorers was one of the
greatest adventure stories of the twentieth century. The two
expeditions undertook an awesome 1,500-mile trek across the
desolate, frozen wastes of Antarctica, facing danger, extreme

suffering and death. Each leader's motives and methods were quite different, but the aim was the same – to be the first to plant their country's flag at the Pole.

Today, in these globe-trotting times, the likes of Dame Ellen McArthur can sail alone to the far extremities of the earth single-handedly while broadcasting her achievements live on television, and it perhaps seems that the South Pole is not that far away. However, at the start of the twentieth century it must have appeared roughly equivalent in difficulty to travelling to the Moon. In Britain patriotic fevour grew as it appeared that Captain Scott was going to turn the race to the South Pole into yet another Great British victory.

Wily Amundsen, however, concealed his intentions to beat the British until very late in the day; he made it to the Pole and back safely while Scott and his team froze to a grisly death in the terrible conditions. Afterwards, a myth grew up that gallant Scott had been defeated only by the underhand Scandinavians, rather than as a result of his own errors of judgement.

Amundsen won the race, but it was Scott who was to reap the glory. After the bitter disappointment of coming second all 5 members of the British Polar team perished on the return journey. The last 3 to die were Scott, Wilson and Bowers, just 11 miles from safety. The tragedy turned Scott into a national hero, hailed as an inspiration to succeeding generations. But the truth, as usual, was a good deal more complicated. Scott was certainly brave and heroic but he was not without flaws and he most certainly made many fundamental mistakes on the expedition that were to cost him and his companions their lives.

In the early 1980s Central Television decided to make a
£5 million television series dramatising this extraordinary
historical episode and, to their credit, they were determined
right from the start to make the onscreen account as honest
and faithful to real events as they could possibly manage. It was
precisely this uncompromising film-making integrity that
attracted Martin Shaw to the role. 'If a film or a play or a
television series is worth producing,' he said simply, just after he
landed the part, 'then it is worth making with the highest
possible standards. I am not interested in becoming involved in
second-rate work of any kind.'

One aspect of Shaw's intense professionalism is his attention
to accuracy. He simply refuses to accept any neglect of detail
and more than once it has drawn him into conflict. 'I've heard
directors and producers say, "Never mind, they'll never notice,"
about what appears to be something very trivial and I
absolutely loathe that attitude. I don't care whether "they'll
notice" or not, but I know that I will notice. That kind of
thinking is a disease which infects everything.'

On 12 November 1912, a search party combing the
Antarctic for the missing British polar team found what they
dreaded most – a small tent covered with drifted snow. Inside
lay the frozen bodies of the British explorer Captain Robert
Falcon Scott and his colleagues Wilson and Bowers, huddled
together against the cold that had finally killed them. Close at
hand were their last diaries and letters to loved ones.

'These rough notes and our dead bodies must tell the tale,'
wrote Scott, in his dying message to the public. News of the
tragedy resounded round the world and out of those last

writings was born a myth. Despite the failure of his expedition to the South Pole, Scott had achieved in death the heroism that he desired in life.

'Scott personified the glorious failure which by now had become a British ideal.' said Roland Huntford, author of the controversial book *Scott and Amundsen* upon which Central's series was to be based. 'He was a suitable hero for a nation in decline.'

The screenplay for the great story was penned by award-winning writer Trevor Griffiths, who said: 'We have all been gripped by the myth of Scott in one way or another. I remember my grandmother telling me, on the twenty-fifth anniversary of his death, that Scott was a great man who had had the bad luck and Amundsen was a liar and a cheat who ate his dogs. This is how the story was logged universally throughout the British Empire.'

Like millions of others, Griffiths had seen the powerful 1948 John Mills' film *Scott of the Antarctic,* which further reinforced the impression that the British explorer was the moral victor of the race. 'All through my schooldays, Scott was placed on a pedestal alongside other British heroes like Sir Walter Raleigh,' said the screenwriter.

'Then in 1981 when I read Roland Huntford's book I realised that the accepted story of Scott and Oates and all the companions who died was based on the suppression of a good deal of the pertinent evidence. At the same time I realised that until now I had known virtually nothing about Amundsen because somehow he had been eliminated from the reckoning in the building of the myth.'

When Huntford was researching his influential and acclaimed book he discovered that some 60 passages and references had been cut from Scott's original diaries before they were published. The cuts were made by an editorial committee chaired by Scott's wife. 'Those cuts,' says Trevor Griffiths, 'were in the main either brutal character attacks on other members of the expedition or tormented self-criticisms of his own part in the failure. Amundsen had steeped himself in the science of survival in the ice and snow. He knew dog and sledge, and ski and men in a way that Scott never did. It is a little-known fact that while 5 of the British expedition died of malnutrition, scurvy and exposure, the Norwegian 5 came back weighing several pounds heavier than when they set out. All I seek to do is to present the whole story again using the evidence that is now available. I think the treatment of Scott in my dramatic fiction is honest.

'I have absolutely no interest in knocking Scott as a man. I see him as very much a victim of his times, filled with inappropriate ambitions which went far beyond his competence as a human being. And I find his death as moving now as I did before. But I perceive it in a quite different way – not as evidence of imperial greatness, but more as an illustration of a sort of empty rhetoric.'

Certainly the realisation that they had been beaten to the South Pole came as a brutally painful blow to Scott and his exhausted team. First they saw something that looked like a cairn and then, as they slowly approached, they realised the black speck was in fact a flag tied to part of a sledge. Nearby were the remains of a camp and the clear outlines of many tracks and footprints of man and dog. The devastated Scott wrote in his diary: 'This told us the whole story. The Norwegians have forestalled us and are first at the Pole. Many thoughts come and much discussion have we had. All the day dreams must go; it will be a wearisome return.'

Even the weather seemed to be against Scott. The next day they were struck by a force five gale and -54°F (-47°C) of frost. They faced dragging their dwindling provisions 800 miles back across the most forbidding conditions on the planet to safety and they never made it. It was mid–March by the time Oates famously said: 'I am just going outside and may be some time,' and stumbled out of the tent never to be seen alive again. Scott wrote: 'We knew that poor Oates was walking to his death but though we tried to dissuade him, we knew it was the act of a brave man and an English gentleman.'

Other members of the team died just as tragically and Scott himself knew his own end was near. Yet while half-starved and three-quarters frozen he still managed to write no fewer than 12 letters to relations and comrades. To James Barrie he wrote: 'I may not have proved a great explorer but we have done the greatest march ever made and come very near to great success.' And to his beloved wife Kathleen he wrote: 'I want you to take the whole thing very sensibly, as I am sure you will. You know I cherish no sentimental rubbish about marriage. When the right man comes to help you in life you ought to be your happy self again. I was not a very good husband but I hope I shall be a good memory.'

In his final messages Scott insisted that the disastrous end to the expedition was not due to poor planning, but to bad weather and bad luck. As he prepared to die he wrote: 'For my own sake I do not regret this journey, which has shown that Englishmen can endure hardships, help one another and meet death with as great a fortitude as ever in the past.'

Scott became an example to a generation of Englishmen. Two years after his expedition, World War I broke out. As one writer put it in *The Treasury* magazine in 1916, Scott had given his countrymen, '… an example of endurance. We have so many heroes among us now, so many Scotts, holding sacrifice above gain, and we begin to understand what a splendour arises from the bloody fields of Flanders and Gallipoli.'

Clearly Martin Shaw had a difficult task on his hands, but it was one he approached with enormous relish as well as his customary dedication. As an adventure-loving boy growing up in Birmingham, Martin had read with enthusiasm about Scott's amazing exploits and he did not hesitate when he was offered the demanding lead role in the production. Until then best known to television audiences for his gritty portrayal of Doyle in *The Professionals*, Shaw was recognised by the producers as an actor of great talent and considerable versatility. Other famous names were considered and discarded. 'We were convinced Martin was the right person for the part,' said executive producer Robert Buckler, 'and luckily for us he was prepared to leave a successful West End run in *The Country Girl* to take up our offer.'

The Last Place On Earth also starred the distinguished Norwegian actor Sverre Anker Ousdal as Amundsen and Susan Wooldridge, acclaimed for her portrayal of Daphne Manners in *The Jewel In The Crown*, as Scott's fiery and independent wife,

Kathleen. Stephen Moore played Wilson and Max von Sydow was Fridtjof Nansen, Amundsen's mentor. Richard Morant was Captain Oates, Syvester McCoy played Lt Birdie Bowers and *Auf Wiedersehen, Pet* star Pat Roach became Petty Officer Evans.

Martin was very enthusiastic about taking on such a different and challenging role but his official response was typically cautious and guarded. 'Scott's character has unusual depth and range which I know will stretch me as an actor,' he observed. 'So I welcome the opportunity. At the start my knowledge of him was pretty sparse but he was a childhood hero to me in much the same way as he is to most English schoolboys.'

As he prepared for his metamorphosis into Scott by reading everything he could about the explorer, he was able to balance Scott's undisputed courage and sense of adventure with the less positive elements in his personality. 'I read a great deal but all the things I read about Robert Falcon Scott seemed to disagree with each other,' said Martin. 'So eventually I stopped reading and just let osmosis and the script do the rest. Scott is usually thought of as being a saint and he was not by any means. I do not believe there is any such thing as an unsullied hero: it is posterity that awards the honours. But it was certainly true that many people on the expedition disliked him, including Captain Oates. But there is a lot to suggest too that Oates was a miserable sod who was constantly complaining! But until you have been out in those conditions you can have no idea what strain, what incredible strain, both mental and physical, they were under.'

The series followed the stories of Scott and Amundsen from their political manoeuvrings in London and Norway as they gathered men and money for their separate, rival expeditions to the drama and excitement of their journey across Antarctica.

At the start Amundsen was 39, a professional polar explorer from the tiny new nation of Norway, who was dedicated to the goal of achievement. He knew that success depended on meticulous preparation and he had turned himself into a survival expert and a practised skier. For him victory could mean future backing for his polar researches. He was calculating enough to conceal his planned attempt on the South Pole until it was too late for anyone to stop him.

Scott was 43, the product of a rich and powerful British Empire already in decline. He was a comparative amateur in the field of exploration who was urged on to make his bid by an ambitious wife and the hope of promotion in the Royal Navy. A fierce patriot, he was spurred on by the deeply ingrained conviction that Britain had a supreme right to the Pole.

On the long journey across the Antarctic ice Scott stubbornly insisted on travelling the majority of the way on foot, using ponies to pull most of the supplies on sledges while Amundsen, who had learned from previous experience, relied on huskies and the use of skis. Amundsen knew he was at loggerheads with his rival. At the time he said: 'The English have loudly and openly told the world that skis and dogs are unusable in these regions and that fur clothes are rubbish – we will see, we will see.' Previous Polar explorer Sir Ernest Shackleton thought Amundsen was wrong and said so publicly: 'I cannot see how Amundsen can hope to reach the South Pole unless he has a large number of ponies on board. He may have dogs, but they are not very reliable.' But Amundsen's dogs were a great deal more reliable than Scott's ponies and the Norwegian was right. It was to prove a crucial decision. Scott's already difficult task became almost impossible as the sledges broke down and most of the ponies had to be shot.

The Last Place On Earth was filmed on location in Norway, Canada, Greenland, Scotland and London, over a 6-month period from February to August 1984. The splendours and horrors of Antarctica were recreated in Frobisher Bay, Canada, on the edge of the Arctic Circle. The absence of penguins was evidently the only significant difference in the landscape. Scott's ship, the *Terra Nova* was reconstructed in Denmark for the production and the three-masted barque was later converted into Amundsen's *Fram* by the judicious switching of masts, deck-housing, stern and markings.

Martin Shaw's experiences while filming in the Canadian Arctic gave him further insight into Scott's motivation. 'My work there was the hardest thing I've ever done from a physical point of view,' he said. 'High winds are the order of just about every day and the chill factor means a drop of one degree for every mile per hour of wind. But though we endured very low temperatures, and worked 12 to 14 hours a day hauling sledges loaded with 200lb, we had the merest glimmer of what it was like for Scott and his men working hour after hour, day after day for months.'

Martin was quick to point out that although the conditions for filming were comparatively difficult, the cast and crew had hot coffee on tap and after work they were all able to go back to warm hotels and hot baths. 'You simply cannot adequately describe the cold,' said Martin. 'It goes beyond cold into pain, and we were being well fed. As I said, the sledges we pulled weighed about 200lb but the ones that Scott and his team were pulling weighed 800lb! And they were living in those conditions for nearly 3 years. They did not have fresh food and multi-vitamins – for most of the time they survived on hard tack. On the march, it literally came down to a biscuit per person per day and towards the end they were falling apart with scurvy, frostbite and gangrene. The agony and fatigue they underwent is beyond our comprehension now, and it was all voluntary. I don't care what his motives were – to have done all that was superhuman, and for people to stay with him! Whatever his leadership is supposed to have been, the fact that they stayed is a vindication.'

Anyone at all familiar with the great explorer might well have at first wondered why Shaw was cast as Robert Falcon Scott. Physically, the fit, athletic actor had little in common with the weak-chinned, slightly balding, fragile-looking Scott. More than three inches of his hair had to be shaved off for the role, which gave him a prominent and disconcerting forehead that was hard to ignore. 'When I looked in the mirror,' he said, 'I thought, "Oh God, this is too ugly and I feel too awful to be seen anywhere." On the rare days when we were shooting Scott in a hat I looked even more weird because I didn't have to shave this great dome of stubble.' Martin's son Luke, who was 15 at the time, was shocked by his father's new look. 'He absolutely hated what I had done to myself,' says Martin. 'He was so upset by it that he would not even look at me. Once I had the make-up on, and Scott's costume, it was all right but the first time I saw my profile on screen I realised just how dreadful I looked – I felt really desperate.'

He was then married to his second wife Maggie, an alternative therapist and psychologist, and they lived in Stoke Newington, London. Maggie was pretty alarmed by the new look as well. Martin said: 'I found out later that Maggie was also upset by the haircut. She wouldn't tell me at the time just how much she disliked it because she did not want to upset me.' He felt Scott's role was 'not nearly as good as Amundsen's' and noted that the Norwegian had all the best lines and all the best costumes. 'In fact,' he said later, 'it was the capricious side of my nature, tied up with pride, that said to me, "I've got to be ugly, I haven't got the best part, it's a challenge – I'll do it."'

However, his performance as the real man behind the mythical explorer soon became riveting, though his portrayal of Scott was never likely to win him any points with those comfortable with the traditional Scott legend.

As played by Shaw, Scott certainly appeared to be brave and valiant, but also an upper-class, insecurely tyrannical, over-emotional ninny. What was so remarkable about this performance is that this was exactly what writer Roland Huntford thought of Scott, and Shaw captures his persona perfectly. It was true that the screenwriter didn't give Scott much in the way of redeemable qualities, but Shaw was careful to grab them when he could. Despite whining at almost every turn, Shaw also played Scott as someone who was into something way over his head – and knew it. He was at his most impressive as Scott near the end, as the embattled remains of the expedition were trapped in their tent – weak, freezing and yet so close to the safety of their base. Shaw's voiceover reads movingly from Scott's actual journal, while on-screen he

Martin played bear trainer Don Demarco in *Ladder of Swords*, co-starring with Juliet Stevenson, where he did all his own stunts, including feeding the bears mouth-to-mouth.

Celebrated for his versatility, Martin won rave reviews from audiences and critics alike in Alan Bleasdale's stage musical *Are You Lonesome Tonight?* He played the rock 'n' roll king, in the last few hours of his life, to sell-out theatres and wide acclaim. © *Empics*

As comfortable on stage as he is screen, (*top left*) Martin celebrates with Hannah Gordon the success of *An Ideal Husband* in 1992, the Peter Hall directed play which sold out on Broadway before moving to the West End. (*Top right and bottom*) The compelling docu-drama *Who Bombed Birmingham?* cast Martin as TV producer Ian McBride, with John Hurt as the Labour MP Chris Mullin.

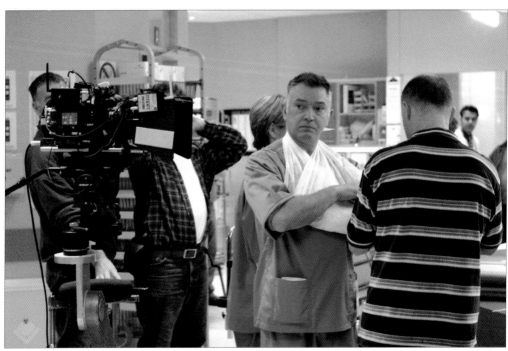

Top: Denise Black, Martin Shaw, Richard E Grant, Julie Cox and Roman Vibert at a photocall for the launch of the BBC's *The Scarlett Pimpernel*.   © *Empics*

Bottom: Martin on the set of St Victor's hospital for ITV's *A&E*.   © *ITV*

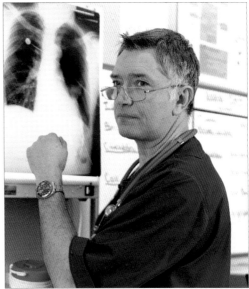
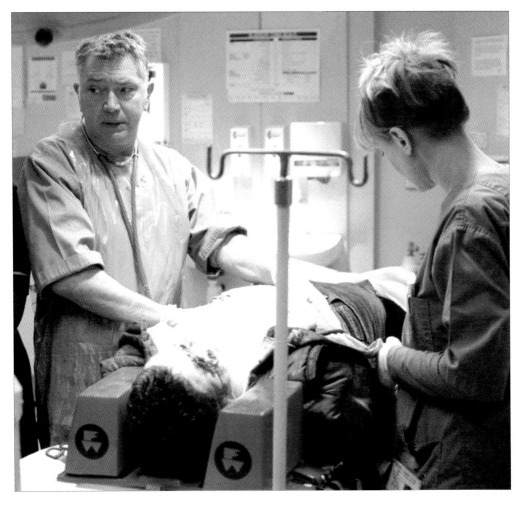

'Always and Everyone' was the motto of the hospital in *A&E*, in which Martin played Dr Robert Kingsford. © *ITV*

Top: A committed vegan, Martin is seen with actress Joanna Lumley during a demonstration to highlight the suffering of animals marking the 30th anniversary of Compassion in World Farming. © *Empics*

Middle: Martin in a camouflaged jeep and the cockpit of a Jaguar at Fairford to help promote the 50th anniversary of the NATO.
© *Rex Features*

Right: Having demonstrated against asylum and deportation laws abroad, Martin protests here against the Russian government's refusal to grant exit visas to Russian Jews. © *Rex Features*

Martin and Vicky Kimm, who separated in late 2004, in happier times with his wartime Boeing Stearman at Swanton Morley airfield in Norfolk.　　© Rex Features

The *Eastern Daily Press* report the accident involving Martin's aeroplane.

© *Eastern Daily Press*

Eastern Daily Press

Monday, August 2, 2004 45p

www.EDP24.co.uk

TODAY'S PULL-OUTS: TV & RADIO GUIDE, SPORT

THE COUNTRY'S TOP-SELLING REGIONAL MORNING NEWSPAPER

Martin Shaw looks on as his aircraft comes down in Norfolk field

TV STAR'S PLANE IN CRASH DRAMA

By MARK NICHOLLS

Television star Martin Shaw looked on in horror yesterday as his vintage biplane crash landed and burst into flames in a stubble field - leaving the pilot and his passenger to make a dramatic escape.

Experienced flier Phil Stead freed himself from the wreckage, then bravely released his passenger as leaking aviation fuel ignited the second-world-war training plane at Old Buckenham airfield, near Attleborough.

The pilot had managed to bring down the aircraft when it developed problems seconds after leaving the runway on a routine flight.

As the drama unfolded at the end of the runway, Mr Shaw watched anxiously from the clubhouse while the airfield's fire crews fought to put out the flames.

Last night, he paid tribute to Mr Stead for his courage in rescuing the passenger and his skill in bringing down the 1941 Boeing PT17 Stearman aircraft so quickly after the problem started.

CRASH DRAMA: Martin Shaw and his wife Vicky Kimm with the PT17 Stearman plane involved in yesterday's accident.

The star of Judge John Deed and Anglia TV's The Chief told the EDP: "This is a strong aircraft and we will have it rebuilt and flying again but, more importantly, what I must do is pay tribute to the pilot for the way he got the passenger out safely and at the expense of himself."

Mr Shaw, who was with his wife, Mr Shaw presenter Vicky Kimm, at the airfield, praised the Buckenham fire crew for the speed with which they responded to the crash, which happened just after 4.45pm.

The passenger, a man in his 60s, has not been named but is understood to have suffered relatively minor injuries.

Mr Shaw, who has a private pilot's licence and lives a short distance from the airfield, later revealed that he had been due to fly in the two-seater biplane on the next flight of the afternoon.

Nik Coleman, the airfield's commercial manager, said the aircraft had been performing well until the crash landing.

He said: "The flight was a normal trial lesson. It is understood the passenger had been bought it as a present, and the aircraft had completed three or four earlier in the day.

"The plane had become airborne but soon after take-off it suffered some kind of problem. We do not know what it was but it caused the know what it was but it caused the pilot to abort and put the aircraft over on to its back and it caught down in a field at the end of the runway.

"Once it hit the stubble field, the impact snapped off the undercarriage and flipped the aircraft over on to its back and it caught"

■ TURN TO PAGE 10

FIND YOUR Q8 CUT-PRICE FUEL VOUCHER ON PAGE 38, COFFEE BREAK – PAGE 23

...ger Worthington City manager his involvement with a community project when he officially opens Holt Youth Centre.

Mr Worthington, who has helped the project over several years, opens the centre on August 19. Young people and adult learners began using the £200,000 "centre of excellence" in Old Station Way in April. It is the result of six years' work by fundraisers and townsfolk.

'Plan for a quieter town' – councillor

GORLESTON: A plea has been made to give the town a planning brief that is separate from Yarmouth's – to reflect its "different, quieter environment", Michael Castle, Labour group leader on Yarmouth Borough Council, has proposed the idea, endorsed by colleagues representing Gorleston wards. He said the move would allow its heritage to be conserved and boost shopping areas.

Elderly couple hurt as car overturns

MUNDESLEY: An elderly man and woman were injured yesterday after their car overturned. The accident happened on the corner of Munhaven Close and Station Road at about 10.20am. The couple were taken to the Norfolk and Norwich University Hospital. No other vehicle was involved.

Stepping out to

Eastern Daily Press, Monday, August 2, 2004

Picture: KEIRON TOVELL

SCENE: The biplane which crashlanded in a stubble field after taking off from Old Buckenham airfield.

TV star's plane in crash drama

■ FROM PAGE ONE

fire. The pilot, who is extremely experienced, managed to extricate himself from the plane and then release the passenger."

The airfield's fire tender was rapidly on the scene with a duty crew member having seen the incident as it developed. He was able to sound the alarm as it developed.

Mr Coleman said: "They were rapidly on the scene and managed to put out the fire on the aircraft and in the field of stubble that surrounded it."

Fire crews from Attleborough, Hingham, Wymondham, Sprowston, Norwich and Hethersett were called in. Paramedics and the East Anglian Air Ambulance attended but neither pilot nor passenger had hospital treatment.

"It's amazing they both managed to walk away from this," said Mr Coleman. "At the time the passenger seemed remarkably unfazed."

The Air Accident Investigation Board has been informed. After the crash, the wreckage of the aircraft lay upside down amid a blanket of foam with the snapped-off under-carriage nearby. It will remain there until checked by investigators.

It is thought the aircraft can be rebuilt. Airfield manager Paul Layzell, who manned the fire tender with son William, said: "When we got to the scene the pilot was still quite close to the aircraft.

"We saw he was OK and were able to put out the flames on the aircraft in an attempt to try to minimise the damage and also to stop the flames spreading in the field."

Airfield manager Paul Layzell.

writes letters and waits for death heroically. By the end, it was abundantly clear that he was truly the best choice for the role.

The filming was certainly a memorable ordeal. At one point Martin as Scott was required to weep bitter tears of frustration onto the shoulder of fellow explorer Dr Edward Wilson, played by Stephen Moore. Somehow, in the difficult conditions he managed it, but the temperature was so cold the tears turned instantly to ice. When Martin's fellow Birmingham-born actor Pat Roach, who played Petty Officer Evans, was required to sink to his knees and keel over in the snow, his moustache and beard had frozen into a solid block of ice by the time the director called 'cut!'.

At Frobisher Bay, a small township so cold and desolate it is many hundreds of miles north of the nearest tree, the cast and crew were to spend two long, freezing months in the spring of 1984. To find an unbroken expanse of snow and ice, filming had to take place on the surface of the bay itself, a 25-mile wide stretch of frozen sea-ice that extended 112 miles to the open ocean, pierced here and there by small islands and giant icebergs. However, to get out into the middle of the bay, the film unit had to build their own road. 'The local Inuit population was astounded by the sight of us crazy Englishmen driving our bulldozer out to sea to clear a way through several feet of loose surface snow down to the ice itself, which was over six feet thick,' said producer Tim van Rellim.

The road eventually stretched for 10 miles out into the middle of nowhere and along its bumpy surface, in the early hours of the morning, drove the strange line of film vehicles carrying men, women and equipment to work.

For producer van Rellim and director Ferdinand Fairfax the task of keeping the cameras turning in sub-zero temperatures presented a major challenge. When Scott reached the South Pole, the temperature recorded there was -22°F (-30°C). During filming on Frobisher Bay it sometimes dropped as low as -58°F (-50°C).

Frostbite was a real danger and both cast and crew were instructed in the tell-tale signs of dead tissue. Director Fairfax succumbed to an attack that will permanently mark a small patch of his face, turning dead white in cold weather. Paradoxically, sunburn was just as much a danger with exposed faces catching the brilliant glare from the sun reflected off the endless snow.

It was perhaps hardest for the English actors who had to recreate the Scott party's self-imposed struggle to man-haul sledge-loads of 200lb per man across the hundreds of miles of crevasses, glaciers and mountains that led to their goal. 'I found it very tough going,' admitted Pat Roach, who was a fitness expert as well as an actor. 'I kept thinking about the extraordinary effort of will that got Scott and his men all the way there and most of the way back, especially when you consider that they were not even on a sound diet.'

Roach was a 19-stone professional wrestler who did gym and weight training for 2 hours a day even when he was on location and he said: 'I was in superb condition, but I know how tired I was after man-hauling that 200lb sledge every day. God knows how the others did it! After 6 weeks in the Arctic I have a good idea of what Scott and Amundsen went through – when I watch the series I shall cry for them.'

The make-up department simulated the effects of scurvy and frostbite in impressive detail, while costume designer Louise Frogley had some of Amundsen's original garments – borrowed from Norway's *Fram* museum – copied in caribou hide and seal skin by Inuit seamstresses.

A cold-weather expert, Yorkshireman John Dawson, now living in Canada, stood by at all times. It was at his insistence that eye-catching red tape was always used to run from Base Camp out to the spot chosen for the day's filming so that crew members could find their way back to the vehicles in the event of a blizzard. More than once this basic precaution proved to be a potential life-saver.

The only creatures not to feel the cold were the local huskies. Although Captain Scott used very few dogs, Amundsen relied on them totally and 70 working dogs were required for filming. They were collected, with their owners, from Inuit settlements in and around Frobisher Bay. Ponies, too, were required for the British team. Scott had insisted on taking only white ponies to the South Pole so white ones had to be brought to Frobisher Bay. They were flown up from the US and stabled in a hangar next to the tiny airport, to the delight and astonishment of the Inuits, many of whom had never seen a horse before.

For director Ferdinand Fairfax, filming in the snowscapes was a novel experience: 'On a conventional set you have walls or streets or objects around which you can place your actors but in the snow there is nothing. It's very disorienting not to have any edges to your frames, but once I was used to it I learned to use the space itself – it's very pure.'

Fairfax was in fact director number three on the project. The first choice, Philip Savile, the brilliant director of many fine dramas including *Boys from the Black Stuff*, was evidently replaced early on by Marek Kanievska, who directed *Another Country*, and later by Fairfax. Clearly, organising such a complex and expensive project comes with many problems.

Stephen Moore, who played Dr Wilson, recalls on his highly entertaining website that: 'Without anyone actually dying, this extraordinary project had as many ups and downs as did Amundsen and Scott on their way to Antarctica. Trevor Griffiths' script was wonderfully textured, it showed how men under the rigid class system in England, and led by rank rather than a natural leader, were inevitably doomed to failure. And yet Scott and his men so very nearly succeeded in spite of it all which makes it such a moving story.'

Moore believed his best acting came in one of the tragic closing scenes when Dr Wilson was meant to be asleep in the tent. He says: 'It was so comfortable and cosy to be out of the cold and wind that I fell asleep in reality. My gentle snoring, which can be heard if you listen very carefully, was in no way a comment on Martin's brilliant and self-effacing performance.'

One obvious problem posed by the snow was the impossibility of rehearsing a scene without leaving footprints in the virgin snow. Complicated sequences were therefore filmed without benefit of practice and it was nerve-wracking for the actors who were under pressure to get it right first time.

At the mercy of the elements, Fairfax had to be prepared to use every change in the conditions to his own advantage. During filming on the sea-ice one day, a 4-foot wide crevasse suddenly opened up at the foot of the camera. A quick alteration to the plan created a dramatic shot of one of the polar travellers plunging into the water. When stunt arranger Bronco McLoughlin was pulled from the sea, his clothes froze instantly into solid boards from which he had to be extricated at high speed and with much difficulty.

It was a tough time for everybody. The fiercer the weather, the more the unit filmed on, getting shots on–camera of extreme conditions that were to make the viewer gasp in admiration for the polar explorers, not to mention the actors and technicians who made the series possible. But Martin found that there were even bigger difficulties of the opposite kind back home after the polar location filming was concluded. 'Working in the Canadian Arctic was not nearly so bad as the scenes we did back home in all the gear, the frostbite make-up and fur sleeping bags. To get the same lighting as the South Pole, they had banks of 5 kilowatt lights, 6 inches from our tents and to cool us off with pipes linked up to industrial refrigerators between takes. And they had to be short takes, before we started sweating and passing out.'

Even before the programme was screened in the winter of 1985 many supporters of Scott and indeed members of the Scott family were bristling with indignation and complaint about a programme that denigrated a Great British hero. Martin was sensitive to the feelings of the family and publicly regretted any hurt inflicted. He also made it clear that he did not consider the production 'debunked a legend' and said: 'Throughout the filming I did my best to preserve the memory of a very brave man.' In fact, he went out of his way to insist that he wanted Captain Scott's son, the author and naturalist Sir Peter Scott, to know that he was 'proud' to have played the part. Martin said that Scott of the Antarctic was a fallible man, who was also a great hero and a remarkable person: 'The tale of his 1,900-mile trek to the South Pole will live forever.'

Sir Peter Scott, who had opposed the TV production, was impressed by Shaw's tribute to his father. He said: 'It is very handsome of Mr Shaw to say that my father was a hero. I feel genuinely moved by what he has said.' He had watched the first two episodes of the series and said he thought Martin Shaw was a very fine actor and he added: 'I think he has captured perfectly the quiet dignity and courage which my father possessed.' Martin was justifiably proud of the production and far from seeing it as a criticism he insisted it was a tribute to a remarkable explorer.

The simple facts and figures of the life and death of Robert Falcon Scott are worth recording. Scott was born 6 June 1868, in Devonport, near Plymouth. He grew up to become a naval cadet in 1881 and by 1891 had become a full lieutenant. In 1902 he was Commander of the 'Discovery' expedition to Antarctica that reached the furthest South. He was promoted to Captain upon his return to England in 1904. In 1908 he married sculptress Kathleen Bruce, and then in June 1911 Scott embarked on a second Antarctic expedition, to study the Ross Sea area and reach the South Pole. Equipped with motor sledges, ponies and dogs, he and 11 others started overland for the pole from Cape Evans on 24 October 1911. The motors broke down, the ponies had to be shot and the dog teams sent back. On 10 December the party began to ascend Beardmore

Glacier with 3 man-hauled sledges. By 31 December 7 men had been returned to the base. The remaining party – Scott, E A Wilson, H R Bowers, L E G Oates and Edgar Evans – reached the pole on 17 January 1912. Exhausted by their 81-day trek, they found evidence that Roald Amundsen had preceded them to the pole by just under a month. The bad weather on the return journey confounded them. Evans died at Beardmore on 17 February. Oates crawled out to his death in a blizzard, on 17 March. The 3 survivors struggled on for 10 more miles but then were bound to their tent by another blizzard that lasted for 9 days. Captain Scott died on or about 29 March 1912. On 12 November 1912, searchers found the tent with the frozen bodies, Scott's records and diaries, and geological specimens from Beardmore.

But even in defeat Scott and his men refused to criticise Amundsen for beating them. As Captain Oates wrote, shortly before he died: 'They say Amundsen has been underhand in the way he has gone about it but I personally don't see it is underhand to keep your mouth shut.'

Martin Shaw is a committed pacifist but he could not argue with the newspaper obituary to the Great British hero whom he had brought back to life again so vividly: 'We owe honour and gratitude to Captain Scott and his companions for showing that the solid stuff of national character is still among us, and that men are still willing to be "killed in action" for an idea.' *The Times*, 12 February 1913.

ELVIS PRESLEY

*'I must be mad playing these parts where everyone
knows the end of the story'*
Martin Shaw on starring as Elvis Presley in
Are You Lonesome Tonight?

When the news broke on 15 August 1977 that Elvis
Presley had died, one hard-nosed member of Presley's
business courtiers who had watched the rock 'n' roll King's
slide into drug-fuelled obesity, was said to have cynically
remarked: 'Great career move!'

During the next 12 months, Presley was indeed the hottest
property in show business, his death having released him from
the constraints of being a bloated and sick 42-year-old man
asked to live up to the legend he had so sensationally created.
In dying, the myth of the slim, hip-swinging young singer who
rocked the world and became a phenomenon could live on
without being irrevocably damaged by the kind of shambolic

live performances that Elvis was giving in his final months when, grotesquely puffed up and heavily perspiring, he cut a pathetic figure barely able to make it through his stage shows.

In the year after he died, demand for Presley records and all things Elvis was colossal and prompted the publication of a number of books about the rock idol purporting to show the 'real' Elvis behind the carefully controlled image. Shocking stories emerged about his sex life, his drug-taking, his gargantuan appetite and strange foibles such as his penchant for firing off a pistol into the screen of his television set if he was either in a bad mood or displeased at what he was seeing. Some of the stories, which made for the juiciest of headlines, may have had more than a grain of truth, while others just trashed him for the sake of a fast buck.

Muck-raking Elvis biographies may have flown off the shelves at bookshops, but to Liverpudlian playwright Alan Bleasdale they were 'smelling of the sewer and the sweat of dollar bills.' Bleasdale was a highly rated and prolific writer who had received wide acclaim for his TV series *Boys From The Blackstuff*. So, in 1985, in an effort to redress the balance, he wrote *Are You Lonesome Tonight?* – a play studying the private disintegration of a very vulnerable Elvis Presley, showing him to be a man who was misused, misunderstood, and a victim of his own success and of the greed of those around him.

Bleasdale had been a big fan of Elvis Presley since he was a boy growing up in Liverpool and he had every record Presley had made. The city's port was the nearest in England to America, and Liverpool dockers were among the first people in Britain to get the early jazz and blues records from the

United States, brought over by merchant seamen. Bleasdale could remember vividly when Elvis made a big impression upon him for the first time. He was 10 years old and round at another lad's house when the boy's father came home with Elvis's first RCA album. When they put it on the turntable and they all heard Elvis singing for the first time, Bleasdale says he was completely knocked out. None of them had ever heard anything like it before. As he grew up and learned more about the singer, he says he was drawn to him even more because he rose to the top from nowhere. In Bleasdale's opinion, Elvis was the only true post-war working-class hero.

It was 8 years after Presley's death when Bleasdale came up with *Are You Lonesome Tonight?* which gained its title from one of Elvis's most maudlin ballads. It emerged as a powerful new play in which, Bleasdale asserted, he had tried to pay his respects to a man whom he felt needed a defence after all the garbage that had been published about him. And when plans were mooted to stage it at the Liverpool Playhouse, Martin Shaw was the first, indeed the one and only, choice to play Elvis.

Interestingly, both producer Bill Kenwright and the play's director Robin Lefèvre, automatically thought immediately of Martin to play Elvis and, quite independently, and so too did the Liverpool Playhouse when Bleasdale discussed casting with the theatre's management. All were convinced Martin could take it on. They were equally convinced no one else would do – as proved to be the case when the show eventually finished a hugely successful stage run in the West End of London.

It was flattering for Martin to command such respect and faith in his ability to carry off the role of Elvis, but to say it would be a challenge would be a huge understatement. *Are You Lonesome Tonight?* required very much more than an actor who could sing. 'When I first got the script, Alan Bleasdale warned me it would take the bravest actor of his generation to take it on,' Martin said. 'After I read it I knew he was right.'

He had much to consider. For any actor to play an icon of the magnitude of Elvis Presley would be a huge risk. It was such a high profile role, everyone had his or her own mental image of Elvis, everyone knew his story and would be just waiting for Martin to get it wrong on stage. For him, the worry was that it could conceivably be a very public way of failing. 'I also knew a lot of people would say: "Martin Shaw as Elvis? Bullshit!" And everyone would come to see an impersonation of Elvis Presley.'

As he turned the pages of the script and read the play for the first time, Martin also came to realise it would be the most demanding role of his life, both physically and emotionally. He would be on stage for all bar five minutes of a production lasting two and a half hours and, as a member of the production team later worked out, he would have more lines even than Hamlet.

It was not just the large quota of lines that was daunting, it was their content too. Martin realised he would need an extremely high level of concentration to deliver lines in which a drugged-up Elvis could switch from darkest depression right up to euphoria in the space of a sentence. The emotional waves and troughs, he noted, were right out of the ordinary. Bleasdale had written a stream of consciousness, which did not run in neat sequiturs but jumped from one mood to another.

He would also be required to undergo a startling trans-formation to change his lean frame into the over-stuffed, corpulent figure of Elvis in his dying days. The most obvious sign that something was terribly wrong with Elvis during his last years was his obesity, which overwhelmed him after a lifetime of starving himself down to his healthy weight before making a public appearance. In addition, Martin was all too aware that he did not have the vocal equipment to sing like Elvis. But, then again, nobody had. Presley didn't just sing from the chest and throat, he noted, he sang from all the way down, like an opera singer.

This all amounted to a role not to be accepted without very serious thought and Martin asked for plenty of time to consider. In the event, he pondered it for many weeks before concluding that he simply could not turn it down. There was a part of his nature that hated to play safe, that liked to take risks and he knew that if he could pull it off, it would be an extraordinary feat. He said: 'I came to the realisation that everything of great value that I had done in my career came through great risk and appeared impossible at first. Signing the contract was the most dangerous and exciting thing I'd done.'

Up until that point in his career, Martin had never taken on a role that would require such a drastic transformation in his face, features and figure and he relished the challenge of changing his appearance, his voice and his build. He did concede, however, in an interview with formidable journalist Jean Rook, that playing first Scott of the Antarctic and then Elvis was fraught with danger. He said: 'I must be mad playing these parts where everyone knows the end of the story, and they're all there sitting thinking: "We already know the answer, now let's see if he's got it right."'

Alan Bleasdale commented: 'Martin is taking one hell of a gamble with this part. I wanted him, and only him for Elvis. It is a daunting role because he has to sing and sound like Elvis knowing that the theatre is packed with highly critical fans. He has to look puffy and ill and behave like a slob yet retain the audience's sympathy.'

As part of his research, Martin spent 4 hours a day taking singing lessons, listened attentively to Presley's records, and he scrutinised videos of Presley in concert and read several biographies. Especially helpful were the documentary-style concert videos which showed Elvis the man interacting with other people, even if the film clips were inevitably tailored to keeping his millions of fans happy and as adoring as ever. The string of largely mediocre Hollywood movies Elvis was persuaded to make by his manager Colonel Tom Parker were less useful in that they showed Elvis in unnatural guise, but he sat through them just the same.

One particular trait Martin picked up on was the self-mockery Elvis projected in latter-day concert appearances, with the exaggerated curled lip of the early Elvis and the infamous hip swivelling. And a filmed sequence of Elvis on stage not long before he died made a particularly strong impression on him. It showed a patently stoned, uncomfortably fat and profusely sweating Elvis struggling to sing a line from the old black spiritual 'All My Trials', a song which gained wider popularity among folk singers like Joan Baez during the social protest movements of the 1950s and 1960s.

148

Elvis frequently included fragments of the song as a flag-waving highpoint of *The American Trilogy* in his last shows. With great poignancy, he would sing the line: 'Now hush little darlin' don't you cry. You know your daddy's bound to die.' Martin scrutinised Presley's delivery of that line followed by: 'All my trials will soon be over,' and wondered whether this was Elvis signalling he knew he had not long to live. He stopped the tape and played the sequence over and over again, trying to make his mind up if this was the case.

Martin found the videos invaluable for his research. He could see for himself how Elvis responded and interacted with people and that's when he started to grow fond of his subject. 'I saw him surrounded by people who were clearly awful,' he observed. 'He handled them gently, with generosity and without judgement, and he knew they were terrible.'

Martin saw the end for Presley as a form of suicide. He interpreted the gold foil used to shut out the light over Elvis's windows as a denial of life; it was as if he was questioning the point of going on living. His mother had left him by dying, his wife Priscilla had run off with his karate instructor, his bodyguards were disloyal and he was surrounded by people who would say: 'More drugs, Elvis? Sure.'

Martin commented: 'He didn't have anybody to say: "Don't do it – I love you, I don't want you to die. Stop!" Six weeks before he died he was trying to sing 'Are You Lonesome Tonight?' He was then right off this planet.'

Like Bleasdale, Martin had his own boyhood memories of the impact Elvis Presley had had on him. He was just 11 in 1956 when Presley shook up the world with his first hit

'Heartbreak Hotel'. He was in his teens as Elvis went on through the next few years to become the King of rock'n'roll, not just turning popular music on its head but setting trends, too.

For a youthful Martin Shaw experiencing teenage growing pains, there was much to envy about Presley. 'I was jealous of him for being talented, sexy, rich and successful with girls while I couldn't make it with girls at all,' he explained in an interview in the run-up to the play's opening. 'I had terrible acne. I envied him because he could grease his hair back. I've got a double crown and my hair grows in opposite directions. I used to dip my comb in Brylcreem and run it through my hair trying to make it look like Elvis. My mother permed it for me when I was 14 and desperate.'

Martin had gone on to like Elvis Presley – up to a point – but the more he learned about the man and explored his life for *Are You Lonesome Tonight?*, the more he found to admire. He appreciated Elvis's 'generosity of spirit', a trait which he resolved to bring out in his portrayal. 'Elvis wanted to approach and be approached on a deeper level, but it was impossible for him,' he said. 'People didn't see a human being, they saw Elvis.' From his research he gauged that although Elvis was cruelly abused, misused and misunderstood by everyone, the rock icon seemed to be fairly philosophical about it. 'It didn't change his basic humanity, but he looked for an escape. He went sideways and so he escaped into drugs and reclusion. I want to enhance the public's understanding of a man who lived in his own personal hell. If ever there was an example of money not being able to buy happiness, that was poor Elvis.'

When assessing Presley's charisma, Martin expressed the view that charisma was something you couldn't see or feel. 'But one of the ingredients is that a person appears to be 100 per cent candid. They give you the impression that you can know them intimately but there's always something that you can't get to. It's the process of addiction really – something that gives you everything you want and you're momentarily sated, but then always leaves you wanting something more. That's what charisma is for me and that's what Elvis had, and that's what I tried to capture.

'My style in acting is to take quiet, economical routes. It didn't work with *Are You Lonesome Tonight?* I became personally involved with the part. Here was a man so unhappy that he threw away the most glittering career of his time. But here was also a man of outstanding generosity. The size of the man's heart was phenomenal. Interestingly, when they did the post-mortem, they found his heart was much bigger than the average.'

When rehearsals got under way, they proved as demanding, draining and intensive as Martin was by now expecting. For 4 weeks, he and the rest of the cast worked through lunch and sometimes dinner as well. Then he would take the script home with him and work on his lines still further, way into the small hours. When he did manage to set his script aside and fall asleep, he found himself so wound up that he would wake again at six and jump on his motorbike to ride around the Liverpool docks just to clear his head and try and take his mind off the play.

He worried away at the role so much that he lost weight. And at one point, when doubts began to creep in as to whether he could manage to get through the play without forgetting lines, he suggested to Lefèvre that the coffee table on the set be made of glass to facilitate an auto-cue machine to be installed underneath to help him out in an emergency. For a second, Lefèvre thought he was pulling his leg.

'It was frightening all the time,' he said. 'Frightening when I was asked to do it because it seemed impossible, frightening in rehearsals because I couldn't learn it, and frightening in early performances because I couldn't get enough breath to push that amount of energy out.'

While tackling the play, Martin rightly decided that he would aim for his own impression of Elvis rather than an impersonation. From all over the country hundreds of youthful Presley hopefuls travelled to Liverpool hoping to be discovered in the role of young Elvis to Martin's 42-year-old dying Presley. Eventually, young actor Simon Bowman was entrusted with the role, which included singing the rocking numbers such as 'Hound Dog' and 'Jailhouse Rock', while Martin would be singing half-a-dozen numbers, largely ballads – but dressed in a bulky padded suit stretching from mid-calf to elbow to play Elvis at his most bloated.

This stifling suit was designed to add 8 stone to Martin's own lean 10-stone frame. Dark hair, a pair of wraparound shades and a towel around his neck completed a remarkable transformation. When Martin saw himself in full Elvis get-up for the first time, he was pleasantly surprised at how convincing he looked. Now he had the look, he had the task of thinking heavy and moving like a big man.

It took him an hour and a half to get ready for each performance. He liked to spend 45 minutes on a physical and vocal workout, and a further 45 minutes transforming his slight frame into the bloated Elvis complete with long sideburns and pudgy jowl. There were gasps from the first-night audience at the Liverpool Playhouse when they first caught sight of Martin as Elvis. With his hair blackened and wearing a mauve crushed-velvet tracksuit over his specially made padded suit he was unrecognisable. Martin reckoned the stifling padding caused him to lose three or four pounds in fluid every night.

Such was the interest in *Are You Lonesome Tonight?* that the 5-week run in 1985 at the Liverpool Playhouse was a sell-out and the critics were unanimous in praising Martin's performance, not least his physical and mental stamina. The play concerned itself with the last 3 hours of Elvis's life. It opened with the sight of Presley's coffin sliding into the back of a hearse with a guitar-shaped floral arrangement suspended above it, followed by Colonel Parker holding an Elvis doll, stepping forward to say that, despite his boy's death, the show will go on. It then proceeds to juxtapose the last desperate days of Elvis with early flashback images of the young 'white boy who sang like a Negro,' who turned the world of popular music upside down. Martin's scenes, including a 'deathchair' scene, were largely acted out in a set built to resemble a pink-upholstered retreat in the King's Memphis mansion Graceland.

'Martin was sensational in the role,' said Pippa Hawes, a member of the first-night audience. 'The play is drenched in emotion, and it was admirable the way he coped with such emotional lines playing such an iconic figure in what is not far short of a solo stage performance, all the while wearing a massive suit to bloat him up. Incredible.'

During its Liverpool Playhouse season, *Are You Lonesome Tonight?* was honed and polished and Martin also then took the musical around the provinces where he won first-night standing ovations whenever the show opened. Fraser Massey, then theatre critic of the *Western Evening Herald*, attended the opening night at the Theatre Royal, Plymouth and recalls: 'What impressed me was that Martin really went for Elvis as if it was a King Lear or a Hamlet kind of role.

'I'd gone along expecting a cheesy Elvis show – but it most certainly was not, anything but. It was a monumental piece of theatre. Alan Bleasdale was obviously concerned how well the play had gone down because he phoned me up the day after the opening night to ask me what I'd thought of it. This was before my review had gone to print. I told him how much I'd enjoyed it.

'Martin Shaw exceeded all expectations. He was then largely known for *The Professionals,* and *Are You Lonesome Tonight?* showed he really could act. I couldn't fail to admire Martin's stamina playing Presley, and he carried off the songs, mainly Elvis's latter-day over-the-top ballads, with complete conviction.' Fraser, now a distinguished show-business writer for *Now* magazine, concluded: 'This was surely one of the great performances of Martin Shaw's career.'

Are You Lonesome Tonight? eventually arrived at the Phoenix Theatre in London's West End where the reviews were sensational for Martin's tour de force. For the first time in his life he stayed up till two in the morning to see what the critics had to say. Without exception they heaped praise on his performance. It proved to be a hugely successful run, and

Martin's performance won him great acclaim in every quarter. Bill Kenwright took a full page in the *Sunday Times* that carried printed excerpts from 20 reviews set around a picture of Martin Shaw-Elvis Presley with arms outstretched. Packed houses agreed with the critics and gave Martin a standing ovation every night.

Everyone connected with the show was delighted, even die-hard Elvis fans. Elvis's UK fan base has always been one of the most loyal in the world despite his never having performed there. Some fears were voiced that they might not take too well to Bleasdale's show and Martin's portrayal, but Martin said he was pleased to find they mostly appreciated the compassionate approach taken to Elvis's tragic demise rather than the purely factual one. 'It's new ground; it's telling a story that they already know without the usual sensational journalistic slant,' he said with feeling.

At one performance, an over-zealous Presley fan tried to take a flash photograph of Martin from the stalls and was greeted with the sternest of rebukes. Martin stunned the audience by halting the show. 'Do that ****** one more time and you're out!' he snapped.

During the show's run, a psychic telephoned Martin and told him that he had been in touch with Elvis Presley and that Elvis knew Martin was working on the musical. The psychic went on to say that he could feel Elvis's presence on stage with the actor every night. This news did not altogether come as a surprise to Martin because he'd already felt that somehow Elvis was watching him. Martin reckoned he had got so close to the man that sometimes he could almost hear Presley laughing.

By his own admission, Martin had known comparatively little about Elvis when he first took the role. But, as he developed what he described as an inordinate fondness for the singer, he had an intuition that it was a two-way sentiment. 'What rocked me most – and scared my intimate friends – was that I felt pervaded by the ghost,' he confided during a visit to Australia, 'It felt like I was getting help, it grew, it was like a relationship – we just got to know each other. It wasn't like Joan of Arc hearing voices, but it felt like that. It was a very close presence.'

The psychic who contacted Martin told him that Elvis was up on stage with him every night. And not just Elvis, but his brother Jessie was there too. Again, that declaration from the psychic meant something to Martin. Jessie Presley was Elvis's twin who had died at birth and was buried in an unmarked grave at a nearby cemetery. Elvis's mother, Gladys, had deliberately given him the name Jessie Garon Presley so that her surviving twin, Elvis Aaron, would never forget his brother whenever his middle name, Aaron, was mentioned because it was so similar to Jessie's. From that moment on, throughout his entire life Elvis was never able to write his full name, see it in print, speak it or hear it spoken aloud without a chiming reminder in his head that he had lost a twin brother.

Jessie had been delivered stillborn and Elvis was the second born. Mother and son often visited Jessie's grave and at around the age of 5, it's said that Elvis began to hear his brother's voice entreating him to lead a good life. From then on Elvis had something of a phantom double, a spirit brother and Gladys rarely let him forget that he once had a twin. Martin's research indicated that in his quieter moments Elvis frequently talked to Jessie. He would lock himself away in a room and confide in him. Elvis's mother never forgot Jessie either. She always laid a place for him at the dining table.

As many observers pointed out, there was a real irony in Martin, who was a teetotal, clean-living, slim vegetarian playing a drug-addled 18-stone, puffed-up man who would gobble gargantuan fried peanut-butter sandwiches in the middle of the night. Martin at 40 could hardly have been more different from Elvis at 42.

As the show's run continued, Martin wouldn't have been human if he hadn't started to feel the strenuous pace of performing 6 shows a week and he recognised that he would have to look after himself conscientiously if he was to maintain the high standards of discipline the role demanded. 'It was the role that took me over the most and the one I got the most applause for. But it was also the hardest; it was the one that half-crippled me every night. I was always aware of his presence. It was a hard act to follow.'

So many things went into producing the voice, Martin pointed out. It was not just the vocal chords, it was the neck, back, pelvis, diaphragm, stomach and intense concentration. He made sure he got enough rest each day, even if that meant sleeping through the afternoon, and he liked to get to the theatre – on a bicycle to keep fit – about an hour before the show started, thereby giving himself time to warm up his voice with a few vocal routines and his body with some exercises. 'Then while I'm putting on the make-up, my mind and body are going through the transformation,' he explained to one interviewer. 'It's like Pavlov's dogs now – a conditioned reflex. I automatically go through the transformation.' Martin's performance was all the more remarkable in that he was nursing a hernia problem, which eventually required an operation.

Are You Lonesome Tonight? reached the end of its 10-month run in the West End only because there was not a single actor to be found who was capable of duplicating Martin's role. That in itself was a measure of his performance, and it fully explained why Alan Bleasdale had told him right from the start that it was a brave actor who would even dream of taking it on. The show's success, however, did result in Martin being signed up to take *Are You Lonesome Tonight?* on a tour of Australia, where it ran to similarly enthusiastic audiences during seasons in Sydney, Melbourne and Adelaide.

Martin's big gamble with *Are You Lonesome Tonight?* paid off in every way. It reminded those who mattered that he was so very much more than Ray Doyle of *The Professionals*. Indirectly, the show also turned Martin's son Luke towards choosing an acting career. While Martin was riding high and touring in *Are You Lonesome Tonight?* Luke visited him in Manchester and they both went back to Martin's hotel suite, whereupon he asked his son if he was hungry and wanted something to eat. Taking up the story Martin recounted: 'We'd finished and got back to the hotel at about 11.30 and Luke said: "Dad, I'm starving." I picked up the phone and he said: "But room service finishes at 10.30." and I said: "Not for me, it doesn't, kid."' Martin then calmly proceeded to order some food to be brought up to the suite. Luke's jaw dropped. 'He was so impressed,' Martin recalled, 'and he said: "Actually, Dad, I think I might be an actor." He was not at all aware of the comedy in what he had just said. I roared with laughter and said: "It ain't always like this, kid!"'

As Luke accompanied Martin on the *Are You Lonesome Tonight?* tour, he was worried that all his son was witnessing was the glory – Martin staggering offstage after a standing ovation, being hustled through crowds like a pop star and staying in the best hotels. That was anything but the norm, he had to tell Luke and his other children who were too young to remember the days when he struggled. Martin hoped that in his playing of Elvis they would appreciate what an extraordinary discipline was required for him to get through it and sustain a quality performance night after night. 'Elvis ruled my life for two years,' he said.

There was talk of Bleasdale's requiem for Elvis being staged in America, but it soon became evident that there would be too many legal hurdles to surmount. Some factions of the Elvis Presley estate apparently made it clear they didn't want people to remember the King of *circa* 1970–77; they wanted them to remember him from 1956. American impresarios were impressed enough, however, to come up with some big money offers for several other projects for Martin, notably a *Dynasty*-style role, which he rejected. He could have almost retired off one particular role, he claimed, but felt quality was more important to him than money.

One of these big money offers was to star as a detective for hire in a major new American series called *The Equaliser*. The financial reward was hugely tempting, but Martin turned it down, perhaps fearing it would be a backward step now that he had successfully moved on from *The Professionals*. Another series like *The Equaliser* might have seen him labelled forever a TV crimebuster.

Martin's loss, at least financially, was another British actor's gain. Edward Woodward accepted the role of ruthless revenge-seeking Robert McCall instead. Martin wasn't to know *The Equaliser* would be a big success but even when it became a massive international hit, he maintained he still felt he had made the right decision. 'I'm fairly philosophical about it,' he said. 'I felt I couldn't afford another hard man part.'

Instead he flew off to Zagreb in Croatia to record a role in an American TV series called *Intrigue* in which he played a KGB colonel. His main concern about the production, however, was not any fear about tough-guy typecasting but a worry that he would be filming in a country with little in the way of catering for vegetarians. 'I'll have to take a survival pack of soups, alfalfa sprouts, dried figs and nuts,' he declared.

THE GOLDEN DECADE

'He's got tremendous bottle. Nervous types transmit their fears to animals and that can cause problems. It can be dangerous, but Martin was brilliant'
Graham Tottle, keeper of Daley the bear,
Martin's co-star in *Ladder Of Swords*

Over the past 40 years on television, on stage and in films, Martin Shaw has appeared opposite an array of talented actors and actresses, but the most remarkable co-star in his long career must surely be an extraordinary fellow called Daley who, literally, stood head and shoulders above everyone else by virtue of the fact that he was a 6ft 3in brown bear.

Martin encountered the magnificent animal when, yet again, he chose a role that was out of the ordinary and would stretch him as an actor in a way he had never been tested before. He was to play a circus performer in a film called *Ladder Of Swords,*

161

which was to be shot largely on a Northumberland grouse moor and inside a real Big Top circus in Newcastle.

His role was that of bear trainer Don Demarco, a member of The Three Ds, a down-on-their-luck circus trio comprising himself, his wife and the bear. The three attract the unwelcome attention of a policeman to whom they seem seriously shady characters – especially when the wife vanishes and the bear dies. After taking off with a new woman in his life and joining a circus to perform a new trick, Don is then accused of his wife's murder. The trick involves climbing a ladder of razor sharp swords in his bare feet.

The film boasted a strong cast, including Eleanor David as Don's wife, Juliet Stevenson as his caring new lover and Bob Peck as the detective inspector on his tail. But for many, the fascination of course lay with Daley the bear.

Nine-year-old Daley was already something of a mini-celebrity having appeared in Thames TV's *Beauty And The Beast* as well as in a pop video. He belonged to a real-life British travelling circus and *Ladder Of Swords* was by far his biggest role to date.

A natural love of animals made Martin Daley's ideal co-star and the two got on famously after being introduced by Daley's keeper Graham Tottle. He listened attentively as Graham carefully explained the animal's traits and how he should set about interacting safely with his furry co-star. The keeper was impressed by Martin's courage. 'He's got tremendous bottle,' he said. 'Nervous types transmit their fears to animals and that can cause problems. It can be dangerous, but Martin was brilliant.'

Eventually he was able to do all his own stunts with the bear, even hunkering down with the sleeping giant, and he and Daley shared such mutual trust that Martin was able to perform a trick he had learned from Graham Tottle and one which would have been beyond less courageous actors – feeding the bear mouth-to-mouth. 'Their mouths are enormous,' he reported. 'But they are so delicate they can take a Polo mint from your lips.' Martin recalled that working with Daley was a joy. 'It was amazing to see how well he got on with Daley,' said one of the circus staff. 'Bears are big powerful creatures and you have to be aware of that and beware of them. But Martin won Daley's respect and, in the end, his affection as well.'

Ironically, even though protective metal discs were glued to the soles of Martin's feet to enable him to walk up the ladder of swords with their blades turned upwards, this manoeuvre was still more painful than any of his scenes with Daley.

The nineties were to prove something of a golden decade for Martin's career, with him taking on work as varied as playing an unsavoury character in an Australian cloak-and-dagger mini-series made in Sydney called *Cassidy*, and yet also making his mark in New York on Broadway in Oscar Wilde's melodramatic comedy *An Ideal Husband* directed by Peter Hall.

Martin has always enjoyed working in Australia, where he has made many friends, and in *Cassidy*, he played James Griffin, a wily charmer who ingratiates himself for devious purposes with the beautiful grieving daughter of a fictional New South Wales premier who has committed suicide. Griffin is the son of a Hong Kong 'businessman' whose dealings turn out to be linked to those of the deceased politician.

Caroline Goodall co-starred as the daughter, Charlie Cassidy, left with a legacy of illegal dealings in this tangled story of politics, drugs and intrigue. The script called for Martin to share a passionate love scene with Caroline – fortunately the two of them got on well from the start, the director handled it with tact and sensitivity, and without fuss acceded to the couple's request for a closed set.

For his role as Lord Goring in *An Ideal Husband*, Martin received acclaim on both sides of the Atlantic. One New York critic wrote: 'If any one performance sets the pace, it's that of Mr. Shaw who, padded out to achieve Lord Goring's silhouette of indolent portliness, is a wonder of wit and common sense.' The laudatory reviews he garnered on Broadway earned him a nomination for a prestigious Tony Best Actor Award in 1996.

Back in England, the critics were no less enthusiastic when *An Ideal Husband* was revived at the Theatre Royal, Haymarket, which had been its original London home way back in 1895. Sheridan Morley noted: 'Martin Shaw's Lord Goring is no longer the look-alike parody of Wilde but a rather more subtle creation: the apparent reprobate who alone understands the importance of being insincere.'

The actor Martin Shaw and the controversial writer Gordon Frank Newman have a great deal in common. They are both vegans, both extremely passionate and frequently outspoken, and both highly skilled at what they do. Newman's excellent 1991 three-parter *For the Greater Good* saw the two combine with captivating success. Newman's scintillating script, which was set in the near future, painted a chilling picture of how a government reacts to the crisis of an outbreak of AIDs, violent prison riots and the threat of a police state. With Connie Booth as his wife and Roy Dotrice as the embattled Home Secretary, Martin played doctor-turned-Conservative-MP Peter Balliol who valiantly tried to do the right thing while handicapped by his political cluelessness and a highly unorthodox sex life.

It was a very suave and cultured-looking Shaw complete with suit, spectacles and neat briefcase who gave what many viewers believed to be a very thoughtful performance. But a writer who suggested it was Martin at his more intellectual was swiftly shot down. 'I don't want to understand things, I want to feel them,' he said. 'You have to feel things here,' he added passionately, hand on heart.

It was a compelling enough drama but it did not make Martin want to hurl himself into politics for real. 'I'm only interested in politics as theatre,' he said firmly to the *Radio Times*. 'I don't protest, I don't march, I don't even vote – it seems pointless. I used to demonstrate and be very active in Equity [the actors' trade union] but now I can't be bothered. I think politicians are all self-seeking, humourless and rather sad.'

As *For the Greater Good* was transmitted, Martin was on stage at London's Almeida theatre in a fine production of Harold Pinter's *Betrayal* which he described as one of the most satisfying parts he had ever played. 'Do you know anything about antiques?' he explained. 'Are you familiar with the old antique dealer's phrase that something is "right"? It goes far beyond the dictionary definition – it means its bloom, its demeanour, how much it is distressed or restored. That's what I feel about *Betrayal*. It's a miniature crafted to perfection, an exquisite piece of chamber music.'

The night of 21 November 1974 will never be forgotten in

Martin Shaw's home city of Birmingham, and Shaw himself ended up playing a role in a dramatisation of the events. Members of his family were still living in the town, and there was widespread outrage and horror among Brummies who had settled elsewhere. IRA bombs exploded in two pubs – the Mulberry Bush and the Tavern – killing 21 people and injuring 160. Many of the victims were Irish themselves but the backlash against the Irish community was instant. There were fights at Longbridge and acts of reprisal all over the city, and 5 Irish immigrants with families in Birmingham – 4 from Belfast, 1 from Derry – were arrested as they prepared to return to Northern Ireland.

The 5 men were heading back to Belfast for the funeral of an IRA man, James McDaid, who had been killed by his own bomb in the West Midlands city of Coventry. A sixth man was later arrested and, following their arrests, confessions were extracted from some of them by the infamous West Midlands Crime Squad.

There was widespread revulsion at the terrorist attacks and the 6 men received heavy sentences despite withdrawing their confessions and claiming police brutality at their trial. However, following a campaign by the men's families, investigative journalists, Catholic church leaders, politicians and human rights activists, people began to believe the so-called Birmingham Six – Richard McIlkenny, Paddy Joe Hill, Johnny Walker, Gerry Hunter, Billy Power and Hughie Callaghan – were innocent.

Questions were raised about the tactics deployed by the West Midlands investigators to extract confessions out of the men, with allegations of police brutality and dubious forensic test results. The case also had reverberations for the British legal system after an unsuccessful appeal and allegations that the judiciary, as in the case of the Guildford Four, did not want to admit to a miscarriage of justice.

ITV's 1990 docu-drama *Who Bombed Birmingham?* followed the *World In Action* investigation which helped to lead to the eventual quashing of the convictions of the Six. Martin Shaw played producer Ian McBride and it was a role he was proud to undertake. 'It was a desperately emotional piece,' said Martin. 'But to me tackling challenging issues is what television is all about.'

THE CHIEF

*'I'd like the stunts to look as realistic as possible but
I'm not wearing that hat'*
Martin on his role in *The Chief*

Pretty, young BBC researcher Vicky Kimm was desperately nervous about the prospect of meeting famous actor Martin Shaw to prepare for an interview at the Pebble Mill studios in Birmingham. He had a formidable reputation, both as an actor and for not suffering fools gladly. She thought hard for a way to break the ice and make sure the television talk would be fruitful and positive, so she came up with a bunch of daffodils. As soon as she handed over the flowers as a welcoming gift to the actor, the smile on his famous face told her this was one of her better ideas. In fact, it turned out to be such a promising introduction that the pair became good friends. 'I thought what a lovely person she was,' said Martin. 'We had lunch and exchanged telephone numbers.' Both were confirmed vegetarians, and they found they shared a love of the countryside and many of the simpler pleasures of life. Gradually, over the course of a couple of years, they fell in love and later married. 'We were just mates for a long time,' said Martin. 'We would talk on the 'phone and occasionally meet up for a meal. Then she came to the opening night of *An Ideal Husband* at The Globe on Broadway, New York with Michael Dennison and Dulcie Gray. I was really scared and I thought, 'I don't know if I can play this part.' When Vicky arrived, I said, 'Give us a hug before I go on stage.' It was a very warm hug and everything changed. We realised it was more than a friendship.'

Martin need not have been quite so concerned about his ability to play the part. He was a big success and the show would run for three years. Meanwhile, Martin and Vicky married secretly in New York in 1996. He told columnist Lynda Lee-Potter: 'We didn't want any publicity so on the day of the opening night we went and got quietly married at City Hall. It was simple, quick but lovely and spiritual. I did the show and then there was a first-night party in the middle of Central Park. Michael and Dulcie were celebrating their 57th wedding anniversary. They were very fond of us and we of them so we just whispered our news but told nobody else.'

The couple were happily together when Martin accepted a challenge that was to change his life in many ways – from moving to rural Norfolk, to learning to fly, to returning to a high-profile part as a policeman that would inevitably revive public memories of the show that still haunted him: *The Professionals*.

Tim Pigott-Smith's decision to quit the title role of ITV's popular police show *The Chief* had come as an unwelcome surprise to the producers in the summer of 1991. The programme was an inventive, high-quality drama and had steadily increased its ratings in its first two series to approaching 10 million viewers. ITV were very reluctant to prematurely close down such a promising programme. Clearly *The Chief* had the potential to run for several more series as Pigott-Smith's performance as the charismatic and liberal John Stafford, Chief Constable of 'Eastland', was powerful, distinctive and well-received. Stafford did not suffer fools gladly and in his showdowns with local authority members who largely comprised diehard reactionaries and political opportunists, he certainly found plenty of them to clash with. Pigott-Smith had particularly tired of wearing the blue serge and silver-buttoned uniform of a chief constable that came complete with gloves and braided hat. 'I am fed-up of wearing this restrictive uniform,' he said. 'It limits people's views of what you are capable of.' The flamboyant MGB-driving police boss was a real hit with the viewers and the producers knew they faced a major challenge to come up with a replacement who would be strong and attractive enough to enable the valuable ratings-grabbing drama to continue. The powers that be realised they required a major figure to successfully replace Pigott-Smith, and they came up with Martin Shaw.

Taking over an established series from another distinguished actor is not something that every leading man would leap at. Tim Pigott-Smith was a household name thanks to his earlier role as the evil Merrick in the historic ITV classic *Jewel In The Crown* and in many minds there was a fear that without him the only way *The Chief* could go was downhill fast. But Martin

Shaw considered it carefully and decided there was still real potential for development, so long as his new screen character was distinctive and different enough. Pigott-Smith was persuaded to hang on for the first two episodes of the third series during which time Stafford would leave to join 'Europol' and an ambitious, aggressive newcomer called Alan Cade would arrive from the Metropolitan force to take over his job. Martin was to be Cade but it was certainly not an instant decision to step into another actor's show. He considered long and hard before accepting the role and he explained his thinking at the time in detail to one of the authors. What attracted him to the role? 'Unemployment,' he laughed, before spelling out his broader and much more positive frame of mind.

With his third wife Vicky now sharing his stylish home in London's Stoke Newington and two failed marriages well behind him, Martin said in 1992: 'This is a fantastic time in my life. I would never have thought, even 10 years ago, that coming up to 50 I would feel so good. I'm 48 now and I'd never have believed life could feel so interesting and vital and youthful.'

He was certainly keen on the East Anglian countryside where *The Chief* was filmed, but admitted that at first he was not hugely drawn to the project. 'Initially I was not particularly attracted, but I was interested,' said Martin. 'I met the producer and the director, and it was their personalities and enthusiasm which attracted me. They convinced me that they wanted the show to tackle controversial and social issues head on. I thought Alan Cade had the opportunity to be a very interesting character,' he said. 'He probably had mixed feelings

172

about leaving the Met to come to the country certainly, but it is an obvious thing to do because everyone wants to progress. He was such a senior officer at the Met that the only place he could go was to take charge of a force of his own. He took over "Eastland" which was a very large force covering as large an area as Greater Manchester or West Midlands, so it's a big, big job he has got because his area includes Cambridge and Suffolk as well as Norfolk.

'As an occasional viewer I had enjoyed *The Chief* in the first two series but I have to say I only watched it because of Tim Pigott-Smith. And in a way he is why am here. I knew if he had played the central character it would be a worthwhile series. The fact that it was a police drama had nothing to do with my decision. I had to assess the whole package. "Who is in it? Where is it going to be made? And how much am I going to be paid?" All of those things were just right and in the end it turned out to be one of the best productions I have ever worked for. I have never been treated so well in my life. In spite of suggestions to the contrary I don't enjoy hard work so very much. I have a feeling of hollow inadequacy and a burning need to get on top of the job. I always find myself wishing it was easy and we had lovely fresh air piped onto the steamy set but sadly life is not like that. I would not have wanted to take over the role from a lesser actor, and since Tim had done such excellent groundwork, I am happy to take over. I never thought it would be difficult to step into Tim's shoes because the characters are so different and Tim and I are very different actors and direct contemporaries

'But it is very important that my character of Alan Cade is a totally different individual from Tim Pigott-Smith's John Stafford. Cade comes with the very clear idea of arriving in staid and old-fashioned East Anglia and shaking things up a bit. He intends to be a pretty dynamic chief constable. When Stafford leaves, the Home Office and the local politicians are all hoping to get somebody they can manipulate and control a little more easily but, much to their horror, Cade gets the job and he is even more dangerous and unconventional than ever Stafford was.'

The producers came up with a method of switching leading men that was both inventive and convincing. Chief Constable John Stafford agreed to take on his top new job in Brussels but before he left he was determined to solve a major corruption enquiry. Stafford was called in by the Met to investigate allegations that crime squad officers in the London force had been taking the law into their own hands to deal with criminals they felt had escaped appropriate punishment. Stafford finds an unexpected ally in Deputy Assistant Commissioner Alan Cade who offers to lean on one of the rogue officers to persuade him to spill the beans about their operations. Cade's future chances of promotion in the Met are consequently bleak and he quickly sets his sights on securing Stafford's job at the helm of Eastland, where he charms the chair of local police authority who was played by Kate Binchy. The authority was anxious not to have a Home Office stool pigeon foisted upon them and Cade's outstanding crime-fighting qualifications made him their first choice. 'But of course if they thought they were getting a man they could easily manipulate and control they were very wrong,' said

Martin. 'I was surprised at just how influential, not to say downright awkward an independent chief constable could be. It was highly enjoyable making him as interesting as possible.

'He is not married, but he has a passionate relationship with a gorgeous French girlfriend called Marie Pierre Arnoux who is very independent, and he simply hates wearing his police uniform. He has problems as a policeman because he is somehow bigger than the job. Because he is from the Met he is seen as a "Flash Harry" who ruffles a lot of feathers and takes huge risks. I think that is what is great about drama, because there is no drama without conflict and the conflict is readymade as Cade clashes with the parochial East Anglians and with the strait-laced and manipulative Home Office. Cade is so dynamic he becomes frustrated and there is a tension in the character because although he has a senior managerial job, all the time he wants to leap in the car and turn the blue light on and get involved. At one point he even lets one of his witnesses be a decoy in a drugs bust with tragic consequences.

'So he upsets his new colleagues because he insists on being at the centre of the action all the time. He is not at all keen on delegating the operational decisions, so almost instantly he is in trouble wherever he goes. That's great!' laughed Martin. 'Cade is very different from John Stafford. Stafford was much more old school and much more methodical. Cade finds him a bit of a plodder, while Cade takes huge risks. Also, he most certainly does not like uniforms. Cade was meticulously researched by an excellent writer, who dealt with police forces for more than 20 years, but even then I insisted on getting directly involved and doing some of my own research. I have researched it pretty carefully as well, in that I have asked questions of real chief constables and real commissioners and real senior policemen just to see how far I can push the limits of this character. I have been first of all thrilled and secondly very surprised to see what the limits are; I met a lot of senior policemen and I very much enjoyed the process – it was fantastic and very revealing for me. I met Norfolk's Chief Constable Peter Ryan several times and watched him at work. He became one of the main models for Cade. He has a similar hairstyle and he has a glamorous wife!'

Martin certainly took his preparation seriously and sat with Peter Ryan through a 3-hour police community meeting at County Hall. He watched as the real-life chief constable fielded wide-ranging and difficult questions from councillors and afterwards insisted the experience had been 'very interesting'. As he put it: 'It's another important brick in the wall. Peter Ryan was a very good reference because one of my fears when I took on the series was that Cade would come out looking like a bit of a glamour boy, who was completely unrealistic. But then I found that most of the policemen I met were incredibly glamorous. One of the officers I visited, a very senior policeman indeed who I went to see at Scotland Yard, was wearing designer clothes and "Gordon Gecko" type braces. His office was furnished like an antique mall and he was quoting classical references because his father was a classics professor. This is not the kind of Mr Plod that you are used to seeing on television.

'In fact, I asked him, "Why on earth are not people like you doing a public relations job for the police?" "Evening all" is what we get while the police have such a bad image. Another copper I met is a visiting fellow at 3 universities. Their style of dress, the sort of people they are with, are what I modelled my new identity on. There is nothing about the character of Alan Cade that doesn't exist out there in terms of the dress, the attitude and the education, the youthfulness of the character compared with the seniority of the post and even the girlfriend.

'It's all there which is really great because when I first heard about it I thought "No, I'll be pushing reality." But not in the slightest. This character is an amalgam of 6 or 7 actual senior police officers.'

Cade certainly got off to a lively start in his new job. On his very first day a massive American gas rig was hijacked off the Norfolk coast and in quick succession he had to deal with an international drugs racket, corruption and an armed bank robbery. 'Police work is not boring,' said Martin. 'But much of the drama comes from Cade's own character. He is liberal but then suddenly he does some completely strange things. He is not above being incredibly pragmatic about what is required, which is where he is dangerous. He has to make decisions that involve the greater good. And there is a whole area of controversy where he uses an informant in a very dangerous way which is not strictly legal and his job is on the line. So he is always pushing the boundaries and he never takes the soft option.'

At this point Martin's eyes narrowed slightly and he leaned purposefully forward in his chair towards his increasingly alarmed interviewer and actually used the forbidden 'P' word. 'It seems to me as though you were on the point of comparing this with *The Professionals*,' he said. 'And for a start I wouldn't want that show mentioned at all because I simply don't see the relevance after 15 years to keep comparing it to every single piece of work I do.

'It's the same question every time. "Isn't this a departure for you?" No, it isn't a departure for me. It's just another part and I'm not precious or sensitive about it, it is just after 15 years the only way I can stop it happening is by not having it mentioned at all.'

'But I didn't mention it,' pointed out the author in question nervously.

'No but you were going to,' said Martin.

'No I wasn't, because I'd already been told not to, but let's not go there.' But Martin Shaw in interviewee mode is definitely not a man to be easily put off his stroke.

'There were 10 years of many different roles before *The Professionals*,' he said with some passion, 'and now 15 years of hard work have passed afterwards. And it seems bizarre to me to have everything said with reference to that one time. Nobody ever says, "Isn't it a bit different from that job in the Arctic?" or "I see your hair's grown back again," because I shaved my head in 1981.'

'But I didn't mention it,' said the hapless journalist.

'No,' said Martin. 'Perhaps you didn't actually articulate the word but you were clearly thinking about it…'

Persuaded to return to considering the series in hand, Martin admitted that his preparations for *The Chief* had taught him a great deal about the British police. 'My views on the police have changed,' he said. 'The only kind of policemen you ever seem to meet in ordinary life speak like robots and refer to their notebooks a lot, while on television often the ones you see portrayed are frequently unbelievably glamorous and driving high-powered cars through lots of tyre-squealing action. And then there are the dodgy ones in the news you keep reading about who make all their evidence up. So I think it is really interesting to see a stylish, educated, smart copper like Alan Cade and I now know for certain that there really are policeman out there who are just like him.

'Cade always likes to get involved. The ordinary coppers on his force will be investigating a crime scene and suddenly he arrives and they'd all go "Shit, he's here!" Then later on in the murder investigation they'd have set up headquarters in the village hall or wherever and everyone is brainstorming with ideas and a familiar voice pops up from the back and the officers turn round and it's the Chief and they go "Holy Shit!" So he is in on everything. And he starts work at 7.45 in the morning, which is a good deal later than I do, of course.

'The senior coppers I talked to said it would be unusual but not impossible for a chief constable to be so hands-on because usually the highest operational rank is commander, which is above chief superintendent. But I am very happy for him to be heavily involved because that makes for more interesting work for me!'

Warming to his theme, Martin was pleased to recall a couple of personal brushes with the police. 'I'm just like anyone else,' he smiled. 'I was on the motorway once and a police Range Rover stuck in behind me. Like everybody I drove extra carefully. He was there for about ten minutes and then he drew alongside me for a few minutes and I could see the two officers clocking me and I thought "How long is this going to go on?" After about half an hour of being shadowed they pulled me over. One copper stayed in the car and the other came up and said: "Are you Martin Shaw?" I said, "Yes." He said: "Can I have your autograph?" I had to laugh, and sign my name for him. But I couldn't help feeling that there might have been a more productive use of police time.

'And I had another strange experience. I love motorbikes and years ago I was in the West End of London at about seven in the morning on a Sunday. I was going to a meeting and it was in the summer and the weather was gorgeous. London was empty and I was really giving it some on the bike and being really naughty. I stopped at some traffic lights and at right angles to me a police car drew up just as the lights for me changed. I thought, "There's no way they're catching me." And I shot round the next corner and round the one after that like lightning. I hurtled down the side streets and stopped at the next lights and I thought, "Easy." I hadn't been there half a second and the police car pulled up alongside me. A large policeman got slowly out. He said: "Nice morning. Sunday. 7 am. Lovely bike. Having a bit of fun. That's understandable. Doing it in front of a police car? Now that's f★★★★★g provocative!" I thought it was so witty I was stunned. I was over the tank roaring with laughter as he let me off with a bollocking and with the usual lecture about what happens when the front wheel spins.'

Martin's love of high-speed vehicles and high-mileage lifestyle does bring him into rather more contact with the traffic police than he might wish for. But at least as a teetotaller he does not have to worry about being over the limit. 'I always laugh when I recall one particular incident of being stopped while driving,' said Martin. 'I had just left Liverpool Playhouse after a show and I was heading up the motorway to Scotland when I was stopped by the police. As soon as I saw the flashing blue light I knew this was a chance for which I had been waiting for twenty-five years. A cop strolled over to me and asked when was the last time I'd had an alcoholic drink. I'm afraid I paused somewhat theatrically, looked him straight in the eye and said, "September 3, 1971." You should have seen the look of amazement on his face… but he still breathalysed me!'

Alan Cade did not have any fancy cars or even a high-powered bike of his own. He just used the official Jaguar that went with the job. But he had a more interesting means of transport that looked very appealing on screen – flying. 'It was my idea to make Cade interested in flying,' says Martin. 'They said, "We need to give Cade a hobby," so I suggested my hobby of flying and the producers loved the idea. So Cade's flat was decorated with all kinds of flying bits, books, maps and model planes and I had my lessons and got my pilot's licence at Shipden Flying School in Norfolk.

'I had already learned to fly a glider for another television programme, the BBC's *Sporting Chance*, which I enjoyed enormously. That was back in 1985 and the programme that was fronted by Anneka Rice. They got Billy Connolly, Suzi Quattro, Joe Brown and myself, and they asked us all if there was something we had always wanted to do. I said that since I was a child I had wanted to fly and they said, "Bit expensive. Will gliding be all right?" So they filmed the whole process from first flight to first solo. What I didn't realise at the time was that I had been provided with the greatest gliding guru in the world. Every time I go to airfields now everyone says, "You worked with Derek Piggott!" and they are very impressed. It really had always been my dream to fly, ever since I was 5 years old. When I was working in Norfolk I had lessons whenever I was not needed on location. Now I've got my pilot's licence for anything up to five or six tons with a single engine, and I just love the freedom.'

Martin revealed that getting his official permit to go airborne in 1993 was the 'proudest moment in my life.' *The Chief* provided the chance and he will be forever pleased that he took it. 'I thought, "I'm not going to spend the rest of my life wishing I'd done this – I'm going to do it." So I did. It was the best moment in my life when I saw the airport on my final test flight and knew that all I had to do was land the plane and I'd done it.'

Martin went on to buy a vintage biplane, a 54-year-old Boeing Stearman. 'I know it sounds very grand to own an aeroplane, but it's really no more expensive to run than a luxury car. If you are buying a twin or a trans-continentally equipped plane then they are expensive, but compared with a car they are not so bad. You could get a really fabulous aeroplane that would take you abroad for £50,000 – which is a hell of a lot – but it's not that much when you consider what you can spend on a car. But the sort of planes I fly are much cheaper. I am interested in the old-fashioned American stuff with the tail-wheel at the back and you can pick them up for £12,000 or £15,000. The engineering tolerances on aircraft are enormously in excess of anything that you can get on a car so they are safe. I don't get nearly enough spare time but when I do get some, then flying is what I like to do. I love being up in the air. It's wonderful to get up, up and away in the clouds, and even flying upside down just for fun. It's paradise, just me, the plane and the elements. Some of the stuff I fly is very, very slow and given that you seem to nearly always have a head wind, it's sometimes slower than travelling in a car because your speed on the air speed indicator might be 90 but the actual speed over the ground is usually something like 60 or 70.'

Martin's wife Vicky shared his interest and she had also gained her pilot's licence. 'She used to enjoy coming up with me,' said Martin. 'Then one day she asked me what would happen if something went wrong. I explained that I was trained to do forced landings and she then asked, "What would happen if you had a heart attack?" I replied, "Well, probably we would both die!" Soon after that she decided to learn herself!'

Piloting planes fitted in well with Cade's all-action character. 'He is not at all your typical type of dull, pen-pushing senior policeman,' said Martin. 'Norfolk is littered with airfields so there is always somewhere to fly. It's bliss. I have fallen hook, line and sinker in love with Norfolk and the remote cottage I've found has become an essential part of my life. I love the space around me. It is marvellous to live right out in the quietest countryside you could imagine. It is in the middle of a wonderful wilderness, at the end of a two-mile unmade road – a bit like a drawbridge. It takes people so long to drive down that I can spot who is coming long before they arrive – and take evasive action if necessary!'

Martin always insisted that he viewed every job on its merits and had no aversion to playing other policeman if the role was right. As evidence of this, after the first series of *The Chief* he did the BBC play *Black and Blue*. 'He was a very different kind of copper,' said Martin of that character. 'He was a tough racist chief superintendent. I played that even though it was a very small part because it was written by Gordon Newman. I admire him very much and like his values. It was a wonderful contrast to Alan Cade as it went from being very positive about the police to very negative.'

The transition from Tim Pigott-Smith to Martin Shaw in the title role of *The Chief* certainly did the series no harm – the audience appreciated the refreshing switch and viewing figures remained very healthy. Martin had fallen in love with living in Norfolk and was very keen to do a second series. *The Chief* was never afraid to deal with controversial areas and Martin's own stance on armed police was mirrored by that of his screen character. 'I feel very strongly that the further we go towards the American style of highly armed policing, the worse it is going to be for us all. I am deeply anti-violence. I understand if you have people on the streets going round with guns you have to have an armed police force. But I think you have to take the line of least resistance. I am fiendishly opposed to relaxing gun laws. I think they should be tightened up now. I believe it is unbelievably horrific, the situation you have in America that any half-wit can buy a gun and go around and shoot innocent people. It is a relic of the cowboy days when there was never any restriction and it was every citizen's "God-given right" to pack a gun. Today it is totally insane. The police in Britain are in a very difficult situation at times and there are situations when innocent people can get killed by mistake by the forces of law. It is very easy to be holier than thou afterwards but the police can be forced into incredibly difficult situations. It is a very muddy situation, but I believe the less guns we have around the better.'

Talking then, Martin Shaw was every bit as challenging as Judge John Deed has become today. In fact while making *The Chief*, which tackled the controversial issue of arming the police head on, he told one of the authors: 'I have a friend who is in prison for armed robbery of a building society. He is due for release soon I hope. Of course, no one can condone his crimes but he did not actually use any weapons. He would go into a building society with a briefcase and say, "I have a gun, hand over the money." I happen to believe that it is not as serious an offence to pretend to have a gun as to really threaten someone with one. Surely there is a difference? If you have a real gun and even drop it, then it could go off and someone could get hurt. Surely there is a difference qualitatively and quantitatively between actually possessing a lethal weapon and simply saying you have one? I can't see that threatening someone with an imaginary gun is as bad as threatening with a real gun. If I were a cashier, I couldn't be harmed by an imaginary gun.'

Martin was well aware that he was being controversial and warming to his theme he continued. He explained that he felt uncomfortable playing violent scenes, particularly those involving weapons. 'Sometimes I found it upsetting,' he said.

'Because personally I don't believe I could ever shoot someone simply in the line of my duty. I have always said that if there were another world war, I would not be a conscript, I would be a conscientious objector. The only time I could kill someone is if he was coming at me or my children, I could never just cold-bloodedly do it. That is where my character of Alan Cade and I part company. I am totally against capital punishment; I cannot believe that even very tough men can take decisions like that. I think it is significant that the police do not use the words "to kill". It is as if they use jargon then it is not really happening. But I believe it is worse for the person taking the decision than it is for the person who fires the bullet.'

ITV hedged their bets slightly over Martin Shaw's installation as the new star of *The Chief* by commissioning a series of just 6 episodes but they need not have worried. Ratings of well over 10 million enjoyed the thoughtful crime series and ITV ordered a fourth series with 10 episodes. Shrewd and experienced drama boss Vernon Lawrence said he was thrilled to announce the commission and he clearly meant it. 'This is just the sort of prestigious, quality drama that ITV needs,' he said, 'one which is popular and achieves high ratings, but also has appeal for an upmarket audience.'

After the success of the first series of *The Chief* in 1990, Martin let his hair grow long for a very different stage role in *An Ideal Husband,* which drew great acclaim. After the demands of the theatre, he headed off to his beloved Scottish retreat for a well-earned holiday. He returned with a severe haircut and highly enthused about facing up to the rigours of police life again.

At the time he said: 'I am very happy to be back playing Chief Constable Cade, and to have the opportunity to work in Norfolk again. I like the direction the show is taking. We are tackling issues which reflect the changing face of the police force. It is not just another police soap opera. The series will be questioning the power of MI5 and looking at opportunities for women in the force.' He went on to explain that he found it particularly satisfying to play Cade: '... Because I like to access those parts of myself which affect people. That's what my job is about, affecting people. There's a part of my nature that hates to play safe – that likes to take risks. *The Chief* was a risk when I took it on, but I believe it's paid off.'

In fact, the new series lined up a catalogue of crises for the chief constable and a string of perceptive storylines which stretched him both personally and professionally. Terrorist bomb blasts in Eastland put Cade at the centre of public fury for failing to act. The police boss found his authority undermined by the secret service and an infiltration by Triad crime gangs sparked a wave of revenge attacks among the Chinese community, while undercover work by Customs & Excise left one of Cade's officers seriously injured. In his personal life his relationship with Marie hit the rocks and a long-lost daughter arrived to remind him of his carefree youth.

Personally as well as professionally this was a very happy time. Martin and Vicky fell in love with the wide, open spaces of Norfolk as well as with each other. 'There is room to breathe and just be yourself,' said Martin. 'I love plenty of space around me and the people are very kind and welcoming. They are not impressed or frequently even interested that I sometimes appear on television and that suits me just fine.'

Vicky developed her own television career with a gardening programme on Anglia Television and the couple settled down in their beautiful old Quaker house, which has a wild-flower meadow and is surrounded by fields. 'It's a small cottage with a barn attached,' said Martin. 'In 1670 the Quakers turned the barn into a meeting house and now it's our drawing room, but we still refer to it as the Meeting Room.'

He described his home as 'modest' but clearly it was the object of much love and affection. 'I am restoring it bit by bit to its former elegance and simplicity,' he said as he revealed he was busy tracking down mullions and saving up for proper leaded windows. But his first plan was to get the stables sorted out and install a large Scalextric set inside them. 'I love boys' toys,' he smiled.

'We have a colony of hens and we are going to keep sheep in the wild-flower meadow – and they will never be slaughtered. Everybody thinks we're nuts because we have hens wandering around the garden, but we don't eat eggs. We have a little sign outside the house saying, "New laid eggs free of charge." I am told they are spectacularly good.'

But even rural paradise can have its problems. Martin and Vicky were both very upset when their pet cat Gingerface mysteriously went missing. Posters offering a £200 reward were pinned up, and Vicky was quoted as telling the *News of the World*: 'We've been crying on and off all week. It may sound daft but Gingerface means a lot to us. He has no pedigree and he's not valuable, but to us he is priceless.'

And there was one small rebellion that lasted throughout the long and largely conflict-free run of *The Chief* starring Martin Shaw. He absolutely refused to wear the Chief Constable's elaborately braided hat. 'He thought it made him look a prat so he simply ignored all instructions to put it on,' said a production executive. 'He would pick it up and put it down, and even carry it around occasionally but he would never, ever put it on.'

RHODES

'My intention with Rhodes is to express his humanity as much as possible, even if it is a diseased humanity'
Martin Shaw on his portrayal of Cecil John Rhodes

As a father to three children who all planned to follow him into an acting career, it was almost inevitable that sooner or later Martin Shaw would find himself appearing in a TV programme or a stage play alongside one or other of his offspring. And when he was chosen in 1995 to play Cecil Rhodes in *Rhodes*, an ambitious £10 million mini-series about England's nineteenth-century empire-builder in Africa, an opportunity presented itself for his son Joe to step up and join him. A youthful actor was required to play Rhodes as a young man, so Martin exerted some gentle influence by stating that it seemed to him it would be advantageous if whoever was chosen for the role bore a good resemblance to him.

He went on to mention that he had two actor sons, Luke

191

and Joe, who were worthy of consideration. Unfortunately for Luke, he was the least likely option, merely because of his age. He was by then 27 and it was unrealistic to expect him to play Rhodes as a teenager, as would be required. However, Joe was only 22 and therefore a much more suitable candidate. With the same high cheekbones and pale blue eyes, he bore a definite family resemblance. The only problem was that he was still at drama school – he had followed in his father's footsteps and gained a place at the London Academy of Music and Dramatic Art.

Joe had one more term to go before completing his course and was on a student tour of the Netherlands when he learned that *Rhodes* director David Drury wanted to see him. He realised something important was afoot when a meeting was arranged at Amsterdam airport, and he was subsequently flown back to London for further meetings and given a chance to look at the script.

Within a week the part was his, but it would require him to give notice that he would miss his final term at LAMDA. The opportunity was too good to turn down. It was no small role – Joe would figure prominently on screen during the first two hours of the production – and no one was more delighted at his casting than his proud father. Martin had only ever seen his son on film in home movies, but he knew he had great qualities as an actor after watching him take a leading role in a LAMDA production of *The Crucible*.

Joe knew the pressure would be on him to deliver and that there would inevitably be whispers of nepotism. He was an unknown quantity, but the producers clearly had faith in him and he would have the strongest possible ally in his dad during what, for him, would amount to a 3-month shoot in South Africa. Before he went to South Africa, Joe was touched to receive a letter from his brother Luke wishing him heartfelt good luck.

Cecil John Rhodes was a vicar's son from Bishop's Stortford who first arrived in South Africa in 1870 as a sickly asthmatic teenager in order to help his father, who was suffering from ill health. At 19, suffering heart disease, he was given a year to live. However, by the age of 30 he had gone on to become reputedly the richest man in the world, and embraced three successful careers as a diamond magnate, a politician and a colonist. Rhodes accumulated his extreme wealth by conquering a vast tract of Africa not just for Britain, but also for himself; but in 1902, by the age of 48, with Rhodesia (now Zimbabwe) named after him, he was dead.

The idea of making a major TV series about the 'Colossus of Africa', as he was sometimes known, had first been mooted in the early 1980s. But it had taken 11 years to reach fruition because of all the political and financial problems associated with filming in a country that had been out of bounds to foreign actors and film crews for so long. But time had moved on, South Africa had changed and now, in 1995, the project was at last up and running, as well as having the blessing of the African National Congress (ANC), who approved the script. All involved heaved a sigh of relief when the project was finally given the go-ahead and there was an even bigger sigh when it was completed! As someone remarked, it had taken longer to make than it took its subject to conquer a territory the size of central Europe.

As usual, Martin had jumped at playing Rhodes because – apart from playing Elvis Presley in *Are You Lonesome Tonight?* – this was the most irresistibly challenging role he had been offered. It would be far from easy to portray a man whom many saw as a charismatic and heroic colonialist; others regarded him as a megalomaniac, racist monster whose exploitation of native Africans and their dispossessed lands was unforgiveable. 'His emotional intensity was unparalleled – he had many of the same characteristics as Hitler, Napoleon and Saddam Hussein,' Martin decided.

Anthony Thomas, who wrote the script, pointed out: 'This was a man who went on to seize over 600,000 square miles of Africa and, at the time of the Matebele rebellion, shouted to his men: "Kill all you can – everything black."' And yet, when Rhodes had first arrived in Africa and set about reorganising his brother's diamond mine, he was anxious to be fair and was apparently full of respect for black people.

Afrikaaner leaders were worried that the TV series would portray Rhodes too sympathetically when, in fact, some likened him to Hitler and blamed him for imperialist wars in Africa at the turn of the century. There were those who considered Rhodes to have been the founding father of apartheid, the inhuman practice of separating blacks from whites.

The emotional contrasts and complexities in Rhodes's personal make-up would tax Martin's creativity as an actor to the limit. And, for white South Africans, there was also another highly contentious and controversial matter to contend with – was Rhodes a homosexual? The script called for Martin, as the never-married Rhodes, to cast longing eyes at young blond assistants and weep inconsolably at the death of a treasured male friend, Neville Pickering. Rhodes was prone to surrounding himself with handsome, muscular young men who tended to be banished from his circle once they became engaged. Even Queen Victoria was moved to ask him whether he was a woman-hater, a question he met with the answer: 'How could I hate a sex to which Your Majesty belongs?'

Rhodes's veiled homosexuality was something Martin would have to address in his portrayal. It would be a thorny subject, made all the more difficult by Rhodes's apparently detached attitude to the relentless pursuit of him by the predatory Princess Radziwill, played by the fine actress Frances Barber. After much reflection, Martin's decision was to play him as a deeply tense and repressed homosexual who never consummated his homosexuality. And as for the politics, Martin said: 'I've not played this role from a leftist or a political standpoint. I have absolutely no message or ideal to express. My intention with Rhodes is to express his humanity as much as possible, even if it is a diseased humanity.'

There was no doubt that Rhodes was a remarkable man, whose life was lived in a race against time and who accomplished so much in his short adult life. He survived 2 heart attacks in his twenties, and by the age of 35 he controlled all but five per cent of the world's diamond supply. He created de Beers – the world's wealthiest diamond company; he became Prime Minister of the British Cape Colony, seized a chunk of Africa half the size of Europe for the British Empire, set off the Boer War, and gave away a personal fortune to finance the Rhodes scholarships at Oxford. Despite these achievements, the script would have Martin uttering a deathbed epitaph: 'So much to do, so little done.'

Shooting began in May 1995 on a vast ranch 30 miles from Johannesburg. The enormity of the project was lost on no one, least of all the director David Drury, who likened it to making three John Ford westerns. The mini-series would be filmed on 30 sets and with the help of more than 10,000 extras. Zulu craftsmen were asked to build a grass-hut native stronghold using traditional means and battle scenes would take up to three weeks to film. Permission was sought and granted to film in the grounds of Nelson Mandela's official prime ministerial residence in Pretoria. Three hundred genuine Zulu extras would be asked to converge on a hilltop in traditional dress to perform the native chants and songs to be used in the title music. There were around 200 speaking parts, but only 13 of those would be played by British actors. And, as the production was regarded with some suspicion, the producers feared that some black actors would be reluctant to take part.

From the start, filming was not without difficulty. On arriving in Johannesburg, some members of the production were jailed and questioned for several hours by suspicious immigration officers. Worse still, soon after a replica of the mining town of Kimberly had been built, a bush fire broke out on the veldt.

Joe Shaw first spotted the impending danger when he noticed a pall of smoke far off on the horizon. Whipped by the wind, it developed into a massive bush fire that came roaring towards them, consuming everything in its path. Cast and crew looked on in alarm at its relentless approach, knowing that professional fire-fighters were some 30 miles away. It took just 20 minutes for the flames to reach them and there was nothing for it but for everyone to do their bit.

The flames first licked at the British army tents and set them alight. About 120 tents in the mining encampment were destroyed by the blaze, but curiously the Union Jack flag escaped unscathed. The flames then inched ever closer to the custom-built town of Kimberly. It was all hands to the pumps – except there were no pumps. So actors, extras, technicians and everyone else on the set rushed to try and beat out the flames with their jackets or blankets. 'At times, you couldn't see or breathe, or know which way to run,' Joe recalled.

The bush fire, which rather curiously occurred on Rhodes's birthday, raged for 6 hours and was later found out to have started after 2 overhead cables collided in fierce winds. Despite everyone's efforts, they could not save the wooden hut that served as Cecil Rhodes's home. Red-hot flying embers, caught on the wind, landed on the roof and the hut was razed. Irreparable damage might also have been done to the custom-built Zulu camp if over 200 extras had not been on the set that day. Gamely they pitched in to help save it from destruction. By the time the danger had finally passed, the hills surrounding the set – an area about the size of the City of London – ended up scorched black.

As if the fire wasn't enough for the production to contend with, Martin himself was hit by a flu virus early on and, for the first few weeks, felt desperately weak. In fact, he needed medication in order to film one scene involving hundreds of extras – it would have been too expensive to cancel it and reschedule. He was naturally looking forward to watching Joe film his first few scenes and was anxious to be discreetly on the set to lend moral support. However, he was taken ill with food poisoning the night before his son's first shoot and by the time his son went before the cameras Martin was vomiting and on the edge of collapse. All that poor suffering Martin could do was to apologise to his son telling him he simply had to leave – he was too ill to stay. Later they watched the rushes together, and Martin was excited to see Joe on screen as a professional actor for the first time. He was also intrigued to note that they had the same body language and mannerisms.

Joe is first seen as young Rhodes arriving in the heat and dust of the big diamond fields of Kimberly, looking resplendently British in his cricketing flannels and boating blazer armed with a book of Virgil for his year off before going up to Oxford. Fresh from boarding school, young Cecil is alive with ideas for gaining wealth and power in a rugged frontier ripe for exploitation.

A much-treasured, shared moment for both Joe and Martin away from the cameras came during a break in filming, when they had the chance to saddle up two horses and ride off together into the veldt. Joe had quickly had to learn to ride, and now he was on horseback trotting alongside his father in the South African bush. Both knew exactly what the other was thinking at that moment – how extraordinary it was that they should be together in this incredible setting when Joe had been at drama school just a few weeks before. His young life had taken a remarkable turn, which prompted him to say later: 'I left South Africa thinking: "Will my career ever be as good again?"'

Martin the family man with (*top left*) Maggie Mansfield his second wife, (*top right*) Vicki Kimm, the Anglia TV presenter who became his third wife, and (*bottom left*) son Joe, his co-star in *Rhodes*. Martin (*bottom right*) scales new heights as an enthusiastic rock climber.

Martin and daughter Sophie played to rave reviews in *A Man For All Seasons* at London's Theatre Royal, 2005. He was cast as Sir Thomas More; Daniel Flynn played the King.

Top: Martin and Vicky Kimm arrive at the 2000 National Television Awards at which he was nominated for the Best Actor award for *Always and Everyone*.   © *Empics*

Bottom: Appearing on the daytime programme *Today with Des and Mel* in 2006.

© *Rex Features*

Martin arrives at Buckingham Palace in May 2006, for the reception given by the Queen and the Duke of Edinburgh for people over the age of sixty who make a significant contribution to national life. He was among actors, artists, politicians and authors who attended.

© Rex Features

Joe was on screen for the first 2 hours of *Rhodes* and won favourable mentions from the critics. He was also able to counter any suggestions of nepotism with a commendably straight bat. Yes, his father had put his name forward to play young Rhodes, but as he said himself: 'They wouldn't give the part in something so major to someone who couldn't hack it.'

Sporting a moustache, and dressed in padded trousers and vest, Martin, for his part, did his best with his portrayal of such a hugely complex man. He dominated the series with a performance showing Rhodes – part ruthless bully, part charmer – bestriding the lavishly filmed landscape, ambitiously wheeling and dealing to gain wealth and power while sparking off native unrest. 'Britain has a craven fear of greatness,' Rhodes says at one point, adding that it was up to men like him to thrust it upon his country.

Unfortunately, in Britain at least, *Rhodes* did not meet with much approval from the critics when it was screened in September 1996. The BBC had hailed *Rhodes* as one of the most ambitious pieces of original historical drama ever made for British television – a claim that was clearly overlooked by veteran TV hack Tony Purnell in the *Mirror*, who strangely thought the most memorable part of the epic was Frances Barber's hats. But it wasn't just the downmarket critics who failed to warm to the series: '*Rhodes* is a stirring and affecting television production, beautifully filmed, but it feels like a work overwhelmed by malice, consistently seizing on the very worst interpretation of the man,' wrote Peter Godwin in *The Guardian*. Inevitably the series engendered heated controversy among supporters of Rhodes who saw the programme as a revisionist travesty and among his detractors who felt Rhodes was a chilling megalomaniac who had been wrongly eulogised.

The poor reception came as a bitter disappointment to Martin. He'd had high hopes for the series, especially as it was a major departure for him from the straight, good-looking sort of roles for which he was noted. 'It was the first time I got to play somebody fat, unattractive,' he said. 'I was very pleased with what I did. But there was so much political flak going on about the production and the BBC, nobody noticed what I was doing. And I badly wanted some acknowledgement for that, and still do, because I think it was my best work.'

Martin was bitterly upset by some of the dreadful reviews, believing *Rhodes* was an opportunity for him to really stretch his acting legs and act. He said: 'Most people in my position get jobs because of their credibility with the public. Sad to say, it is not always the best of us who are working. I never assume I am necessarily the best person for the job – there are always ten others who could do it as well, if not better. But with *Rhodes* I thought I gave a bloody good performance and I was confused by the reception.'

The series was much better received outside the UK however, especially in America where a New York critic noted: '… in Martin Shaw's nuanced and compelling portrayal, he is the sort of chap you have to hate yet may find yourself rooting for a little…'

PIMPERNEL

'Martin is a class act. You have to be really on your game all the time because he is so very good'
Elizabeth McGovern, Martin's co-star in *The Scarlet Pimpernel*

'Who wants to be a hero, when playing the villain is so much fun?' That was Martin Shaw's reaction to being asked to play the devious Citizen Chauvelin in the BBC's big-budget adaptation of Baroness Orczy's classic novel *The Scarlet Pimpernel*. Martin was delighted to be the bad guy set against Richard E Grant's distinctly camp version of the Pimpernel.

The Scarlet Pimpernel is one of those classic historical novels that used to thrill almost all adventure-seeking schoolboys and girls with its breathtaking narrative of heroics and romance in the turbulent times of the French Revolution. The story of recklessly brave Sir Percy Blakeney, who effortlessly changed identity to become the elusive Pimpernel and to rescue innocent French aristocrats, helping them to safety in Britain has been a favourite through the ages. But in twentieth-century Birmingham, a teenage Martin Shaw was left distinctly underwhelmed. 'I was not impressed by the book,' he recalled. 'It stretched the credibility a little too far and I could never quite accept having a hero called Percy!'

However, when the BBC came to revive Baroness Orczy's famous tale in the late 1990s, a grown-up Shaw was fascinated by the project – but only if he could play the villain of the piece, not foppish, prancing Percy. The clever, cold-blooded Citizen Chauvelin was the ruthless head of the secret police and one of Robespierre's most trusted aides. Such was his devotion to revolution and willingness to enforce The Terror, he was determined to separate Percy's head from the rest of his body at the earliest possible opportunity.

There have been a whole string of screen versions of *The Scarlet Pimpernel,* with Leslie Howard perhaps the most memorable in the title role of Alexander Korda's 1934 priduction, but the character of Chauvelin was always a good deal more forgettable. Raymond Massey played the role in the 1934 film version as a walking sneer apparently devoid of personality. 'I found Chauvelin very one-dimensional in the book,' admitted Martin. 'But if I was going to play him, I was determined to make him interesting. Fortunately the producers agreed and we worked on developing his somewhat inconvenient love for the beautiful Marguerite, who just happens to be the wife of Sir Percy.'

The lavish £5-million project intended to provide a tough new look to the familiar tale with the producers planning to inject pace, style and the up-to-the-minute production values of a modern action thriller. In fact, The Scarlet Pimpernel was in many ways the first of a whole raft of highly popular dual-identity heroes, such as Zorro and the Saint. 'With all his disguises and rescues, the Pimpernel was really like the first crusader or the first Superman,' said enthusiastic Delia Fine, vice president for film, drama and the performing arts of the American co-producers A&E. 'When you put the combination of adventure and romance against the horrors of the French Revolution it stands the test of time.'

Richard E Grant was seen as a slightly unconventional choice for the lead, intended to give Sir Percy a sardonic charm to go with his double life as aristocrat and maverick. The anarchic and recklessly brave trickster was to revel in his twin personality of mysterious hero and upper-class twit. Behind the blasé façade that he presented to the world was a man of action who really enjoyed living on the edge. This Pimpernel was to make audiences laugh as well as gasp at his nerve and impudence. He courageously risked his life to save as many people as he could from the bloodbath of Revolutionary terror but he was betrayed to cold-hearted Chauvelin, who tortured him to try to reveal the names of the other members of his secret organisation, though of course Sir Percy said nothing. He escaped back to England and prepared to lead more daring escapes but he was haunted by the suspicion that his beautiful wife Marguerite was a spy for Chauvelin. She had been a famous actress in Paris before the Revolution and for a time had been a mistress of the secret police chief – and she was being blackmailed by her former lover. Traditionally the story was portrayed as simply good versus evil but this time there was a more subtle approach with many shades of grey between the black-and-white extremes.

For perhaps the first time in the long history of filming *The Scarlet Pimpernel,* sinister Chauvelin was made into a compelling and attractive figure. In the firm and capable hands of Martin Shaw he became dashing, as well as devious and sexy and sinister. He bedded beautiful women and used the passion between him and Marguerite to draw the Pimpernel into a trap. 'It provides conflict,' explained Martin on location in Prague, which was doubling for, 'And you can't have drama without some conflict – it's almost the definition of drama.' He laughed off the suggestion that he had also made Chauvelin into a sexy villain. 'If I have, I can assure you it is quite accidental,' he smiled. 'Chauvelin is determined to unmask the Pimpernel and send him to the guillotine. I wanted him to be so bad that the audience boos him. Villains are always so much more interesting than the good guys anyway, and you can get to exorcise your own demons that way – it's cheap therapy!'

He was also most concerned to make his character believable. 'If Chauvelin becomes simply a 'motiveless malignity' then he instantly ceases to be interesting, let alone compelling,' said Martin. 'I see him more as a powerful man doing a very difficult job in extraordinary times. The French Revolution altered the whole world order. Indeed, some of its impact is still reflected today in the politics of Europe. We tried hard to get across how enormously things changed in France. I found myself enjoying some of the research and educating myself along the way and the more I got involved, the more I found sympathy with Chauvelin. He does have a desperately awful job to do but he does have a softer, gentler side. It's just that as head of the secret police he has some very unpleasant tasks to perform. This was a remarkable time in history. Chauvelin and the men of the Revolution believed their cause was just and that interfering aristocrats like Sir Percy Blakeney had to be dealt with. But I also believe that Chauvelin has real feelings for Marguerite. After all, she is French like him and he tries to use their relationship for his own ends certainly, but he does care for her. He used to be in love with her before Sir Percy stole her away. He is bitter and twisted about it, and it certainly adds an edge to his relationship with Percy when he eventually discovers he is the Pimpernel. But most important of all is that Chauvelin is not a heartless monster otherwise the whole thrust of the drama is undermined.'

American actress Elizabeth McGovern, who burst to fame as a teenager in Robert Redford's film *Ordinary People*, starred as Marguerite. She was then living with her young family in London and joked: 'Not many people go from Hollywood to Hammersmith.' After her role as the girl caught up in a moving family drama, playing the complex, Rousseau-quoting actress was a great opportunity for her to get inside the head of a person in a grown-up relationship. 'It's about people who have passions and go for it. It's not about people who sit around and think. Marguerite has moved on from Chauvelin to Percy, but I think there is still a small part in her heart for her former French lover. I was very lucky to get two fine and very different actors to work with. Martin is a class act – you have to be really on your game all the time because he is so very good. Working with him was a great experience. I learned a lot and I laughed a lot as well.'

Once extremely agile, Martin was still very fit but he found some of the action scenes a bit of a chore. 'I didn't mind hurling myself about in *The Professionals*, but it is not so easy these days,' he said. With the tiled roofs and cobbled streets of Prague doubling for eighteenth-century Paris, the producers were keen to make all the sequences as realistic as possible. 'It was a bit of a pain tumbling off a horse onto the hard ground,' said Martin. 'The horses were all right because they had special rubber shoes to protect their hooves, but no one thought to give me any extra protection! I am keen on horse riding, but I was out of practice. On hard ground, where you have got guns going off as well, it makes it even more difficult. But the riding master Steve Dent really knew his business and it was fine. During Chauvelin's pursuit of the Pimpernel, I had to chase him through narrow streets and alleyways, galloping at high speed, but we managed it all and I am happy to say that I did most of my own stunts, such as they were. At my age I don't like to fall over – it hurts too much!'

Yet after production had finished, Martin insisted he had really enjoyed the experience. He said that playing the sinister bad guy in a classic tale like *The Scarlet Pimpernel* was: 'Just about the most fun you can have with your clothes on. There's something about costume drama and villainy that mix beautifully.'

On a personal level he was keen to emphasise that this had

been a very happy point in his life. His six-year-long love affair with Vicky Kimm had become his third marriage and the couple were very happy in their lovely Norfolk home. Never too quick to reveal his emotions, Martin was relaxed enough to recall that meeting Vicky back in Birmingham was one of the most fortunate encounters of his life. 'It was the start of a love affair,' he smiled. 'We got married very quietly and now we couldn't be happier.' He was particularly thrilled that Vicky shared his love of flying. 'And she is a much better pilot than me,' he admitted frankly. 'We both love the peace and freedom up there in the skies. There is nothing better than soaring through the clouds in my antique plane.'

Interviewed in Prague, he also revealed one small grumble – he desperately wanted to become a granddad. 'It's a very strange feeling that has kind of caught up with me gradually,' he said. 'My kids, actors all of them, are in their twenties now, but they have still not made me a grandfather yet. And I wish they would hurry up!' The 53-year-old father of three warmed to his theme as he gazed out of the window at families with young children wandering around in the Prague sunshine. 'Being a grandparent is the perfect set-up,' he said. 'You can have all the fun, but as soon as you start to feel tired you can say, "Oi, you lot, go back to mummy and daddy!" The first years of my own children's lives seemed to flash by so quickly I don't think I really had time to appreciate them. I always seemed to be so busy trying to carve out my career that I know I did not spend enough time being a dad. Then all of a sudden they were teenagers and becoming independent and those precious early years have gone. I know it's the same for everyone but life doesn't half flash past you, especially when you're busy. Grandchildren will be simply wonderful and even if it makes me sound ancient, I don't care. I can hardly wait.'

Martin stayed in an elegant Prague city-centre flat for *The Scarlet Pimpernel*, while the rest of the crew were billeted in a modern hotel in the suburbs. 'I do like my own space,' he said. 'But I wanted to have a flat because I found last time I came to Czechoslovakia that vegetarian food was pretty hard to find. That was back in the 1960s when huge hunks of meat were widely available and seemed to make up just about every meal including breakfast. That's not for me, so I got a flat so I could cater for myself. But then I found that Prague has improved enormously when it comes to healthy eating. There are vegetarian restaurants and you're no longer looked at as if you have just arrived from another planet if you don't eat meat!'

Some other surprises were not quite so welcome, however. Martin found that *The Professionals* was still being screened on Czech television and one morning, as he headed for the set he was spotted by a delighted young fan who raced towards him screaming 'Bodie, Doyle – Bodie, Doyle!' at the top of his voice. 'Even I had to laugh at that,' said Martin. 'I was gobsmacked to discover they are still watching *The Professionals* over here. It's a fascinating country and the people are mainly warm and very kind. They can't do enough for you. It was a bit embarrassing on set when people kept fetching me chairs to sit on. I am not at all sure how old they thought I must be! But they followed me round asking if they could do the least little thing for me. It was very humbling. And again it was so incredibly different from my earlier visit years ago when the place was swarming with armed guards. It was so different this time. The Czechs are wonderful people. Their freedom is so recent that they are like hostages who have just been released. They can't help it if they're still inflicted with *The Professionals*!'

A & E

'I was bed-bound and could only lie down but even that was agony.
I really thought I was dying'
Martin on being knocked off his bike

For a committed pacifist, Martin Shaw has an unhappy knack of landing himself in rather more than his share of battles. Perhaps it's because he has a highly developed sense of right and wrong that he does seem to find himself in confrontations too often for comfort. It was on 21 August 1997, when he was cycling to the Haymarket Theatre in London's Piccadilly to appear in a matinee performance of *An Ideal Husband,* that he first clashed with the driver of one of the capital's many tourist buses. Martin was going round a busy roundabout when he was forced to swerve and take evasive action as the bus, carrying Japanese tourists, cut in on him after overtaking. He tried to catch up with the bus and shouted at the driver to protest about his conduct behind the wheel, but was again forced to swerve out of the way as the bus swept narrowly past him. Presumably to make his point that he was not about to be lectured on matters of road manners by a mere cyclist the driver hurled a partly eaten cheese sandwich at Martin as he overtook.

This was unacceptable behaviour to Martin. He chased after the bus in an attempt to take its registration number. The bus came to a halt outside the Grosvenor Hotel on Park Lane where Martin stood in front of the vehicle, still on his bicycle. At Horseferry Road magistrates court almost a year later, he gave evidence: 'I said to him, "Do you remember me?" I was still astride my bike, holding the handlebars. The next thing that happened was that he jumped out of his cab with extraordinary speed, ran towards me and hit me on the chin. I dropped the bicycle and retreated towards the pavement. He followed me very fast and started kicking me on both sides of my body. Hard kicks landed on my ribs, which were damaged on both sides. I just tried to block the blows. I was shouting, "Somebody call the cops!" and, thank goodness, somebody did.' The Japanese tourists on the bus watched the incident in horror.

By the time the police arrived the driver, 28-year-old William Kavanagh had fled the scene but was arrested a month later when he insisted that Martin Shaw had been the aggressor. Fortunately for Martin, a witness supported his version of events. The publicity which followed the attack, with colourful descriptions of the 'ex-Professional' having to contend for the first time with a cheese sandwich as 'a new weapon in the arsenal of fear' attempted to highlight the humour of the situation but for Martin this was certainly no joke.

Kavanagh was described as having eyes bulging and a face twisted with rage. Martin was left with cracked ribs and needing stitches in his badly-cut chin but in the best show-business tradition the show went on and, still in a state of shock, he completed the performance of the play on the day of the attack. The endless references to his days as Ray Doyle, hurling himself athletically over car bonnets and brutally battling villains in *The Professionals*, were inevitable. In court he said: 'I know we did a lot of fighting in *The Professionals* but that was just a show and was more than 20 years ago. I am not a young man any more. I do a martial art that involves kicking and punching but I am just a beginner, a yellow belt. It helped me to block some of the blows, but not enough.' Kavanagh, who had been a tour driver for 6 years, was convicted of assault and bailed, pending sentencing reports. Charitably, Martin insisted he did not want a prison sentence for the man who attacked him in the headline-hitting 'road rage' incident. 'I would be very sorry if he goes to jail,' said Martin. 'I see a man there and feel compassion.' But magistrate Geoffrey Breen told Kavanagh sternly: 'I am considering a sentence of imprisonment. I don't want you to be under any illusions about that, because you were on a bus with tourists on it and ought to have known better than to have involved yourself in an incident like this.' Kavanagh later received a 28-day sentence, but by then his victim's life had moved on and Martin Shaw was about to star in a medical drama. And if Shaw looked instantly at home in hospital then perhaps that is not surprising because he has painful experience of being a patient. As his role in the new show was launched, the court case involving the road rage was still fresh in the public mind. He ruefully recalled his injuries and said: 'No one stepped in to help – they never do, do they? What really scared me though was seeing the bus coming straight for me. Going to prison was a high price to pay, though. It's all water under the bridge now and I wish him well.'

Martin Shaw is used to being in demand as an actor. For a long time now he has been offered many more parts than he could ever have the time or energy to play. So he has become necessarily selective. But he's big enough to accept that he is not always right. One television series that narrowly escaped his ruthless axe was the highly popular ITV1 show *Always And Everyone* (which became forever abbreviated to *A & E*) – and only because his wife Vicky Kimm was listening in on a phone call.

Martin smiled as he recalled: 'I was talking to my agent when Vicky shouted from the kitchen, "What are you turning down?" I said, "Just another medical drama." But thank God she persuaded me to read it, because it was so different and imaginative.' And so he accepted the role as the gifted, yet disillusioned Dr Robert Kingsford in ITV's popular medical *A & E* and he was quickly a hit with the viewers. Some compared him favourably to George Clooney's portrayal of Dr Ross on the American medical show *ER* but Martin wisely sidestepped any discussion on middle-aged pin-ups and instead preferred to concentrate on the programme.

There was no grand treatment for the new leading man. Martin was perfectly happy to be a team player in the ensemble piece and his tiny dressing room was one corner of a

Portakabin in the huge former factory building that housed the fictional St Victor's Hospital. 'Our set was absolutely brilliant,' he said. 'In fact, I found everything about it very, very convincing. You have to pinch yourself to make sure you're not really in hospital. The only thing missing is the smell! You occasionally get good one-off specials or films about hospitals, but in my humble experience it is very rare to find something as good as this – the writing is of the very best quality.'

This was high praise indeed from a man not famous for being easy to please. Martin approached the role with his usual fixation on detail and insisted how every small component of every part is really very important to him. He can be demanding and always asks an awful lot of questions because he needs to know the answers before he can really get inside the head of the character he is playing. 'At the end of the day I want it to look real,' he said. 'For example, they first suggested Dr Kingsford wore Timberland shoes, but when I asked the consultant I was shadowing at Hope Street Hospital in Manchester about this he just burst out laughing and said, "At the end of the day I am covered in half the body fluids in Manchester. It would waste hundreds of pounds of my hard-earned money if I wore Timberlands."' So that's why Dr Kingsford wore cheap trainers.

Martin and the rest of the cast were deeply impressed by the dedication of the real-life doctors and nurses they met. 'Some of them are truly inspirational people,' said Martin. 'They all do a demanding and difficult job at the best of times but considering they generally manage to be cheerful and uplifting as well I think they are mostly pretty remarkable people. We tried to show that on the series. There might sometimes have been a little heightened reality but extraordinary things happen in real hospitals every day. I am very proud of *A & E*.'

Martin enjoyed playing a medical man and he was grateful for Vicky's initial enthusiasm. 'It was exactly what I wanted at the time, a new script that was interesting and different. I get to be Jack the lad and I get to have time off because it's an ensemble piece. It looked like it was as good as it got, and I took it. There is something about playing characters with skills you don't have, like a person like Dr Kingsford who can do amazing things like reviving someone who is clinically dying – it allows you to vicariously enjoy all those skills.'

Martin certainly enjoyed being the caring consultant but he admitted: 'I don't think I could be a doctor in real life because I am wary of the way they don't accept any alternative. I have been learning about complementary medicine for more than 30 years and homeopathy is a part of my life. I have learned an awful lot about things like flower essences. When alternative medicine works, doctors tend to dismiss it. But my opinion is that the criteria you must consider is simply – does it work or doesn't it? I know when I have been working hard and not having enough time for a proper sleep I have often found vitamin supplements and natural remedies have helped when I've been totally exhausted.'

He believes the problem with both alternative and conventional medicine is that each side tends to think they are mutually exclusive. 'Which they are not,' says Martin. 'Conventional medicine is brilliant at carpentry and plumbing. If I had a broken bone or my intestines were hanging out, I would not go to a naturopath but for a great many physical illnesses complementary medicine is by far the best thing and sometimes, as I have found, you can combine the two.' *A & E* was one medical programme which really prided itself on authenticity and Martin, along with the rest of the cast, would always carefully check his scenes with the programme's medical adviser. His three-year spell in *A & E* was the longest he had spent in any part since his spell in *The Professionals* in the 1970s and he confessed that he did sometimes worry about becoming typecast. 'Before *The Professionals* I would go to auditions and be told they liked me but they needed a big name,' he said. 'Then, after *The Professionals*, they would tell me I was exactly right, but I was too well known. There is a whole generation that grew up with *The Professionals* and it has developed almost cult status, but I don't feel proud of it. I trained as a craftsman and as an artist and neither was evident in *The Professionals*. There is nothing to feel proud of other than that I stuck it out.'

And even in *A & E* he was not safe from gun-toting thugs. The hospital series decided to return with a real bang at the start of the second series – Robert Kingsford found himself staring down the barrel of a gun being wielded by a man seeking revenge on a patient who he blames for the death of his son. It provided a tense introduction for new junior doctor Danny Barton, played by James Murray, but it was consultant Robert Kingsford who got shot. 'It was a pretty terrifying ordeal for him,' said Martin. 'They are locked away in a side ward and held at gunpoint by this angry guy. Robert tries to reason with the man, to talk their way out of the siege but the

test

gunman pulls the trigger.' In true hard-man style Robert brushes off the injury as "just a scratch" but Martin was not sure that he would be able to be nearly so composed. 'I have no idea what I would do in a situation like that,' he said. 'The horrifying reality is that this sort of thing does happen in hospitals and the lives of medical staff are put in jeopardy when they are trying to do their job.'

The writers certainly piled on the tragedy for Kingsford. His girlfriend was killed in a car accident and he was left looking after their toddler son Harry while his relationships with beautiful young Sunita – played by Parminder Nagra who would go on to star in the US hospital drama *ER* – and with fellow consultant Christine hit trouble. And child-minder Julie found little Harry too boisterous to care for, so Robert was left holding the baby.

'What I really find incredible,' says Martin, 'is that there are people who do the job Robert Kingsford does for real. Some people have to make life and death decisions as part of their daily routine. I am not sure I could ever do that.'

But the physical suffering from the bus incident was nothing compared with an earlier injury that Martin suffered when he was sent flying after a taxi knocked him off his bike in 1990. Playing a television doctor evidently prompted Martin to speak for the first time about the desperately grim medical ordeal he had suffered years earlier. It came at a time when Martin had no loving partner to nurse him, so his brother Jem put his own life on hold to come round and nurse him back to health. The collision had left Martin crippled with pain and unable to walk for three months because of damage to his spine. Indeed, it was so traumatic that he kept quiet about it until years later. At first he tried to carry on working as normal after the terrible crash, but instead of getting better, the pain steadily escalated and got so bad that he could no longer even walk.

'It was pretty bad,' said Martin. 'It reached the point where I had to crawl across the floor on all fours to use the toilet. I was bed-bound and could only lie down but even that was agony. I really thought I was dying. The pain was worse than anything I have ever experienced before or since. To be unable to walk, stand or sit and to be in so much agony, I thought, "Well, this must be it."'

At the time, Martin was taking so many painkillers that he found himself just lying in bed and watching the time tick by until he had to take the next pill. 'I was supposed to take them every four hours but I was taking them sooner because I couldn't wait.' He winced at the memory. By the time he went to the hospital for a diagnosis he was well and truly terrified. 'They found that some discs in my back had ruptured as a result of the crash,' he said. 'Fluid was leaking, which then hardened and trapped the nerves around it.' The injuries were so severe that he had to have an operation that left him with a 5-inch scar at the base of his spine.

'It is a fairly standard procedure but there is always a risk when you are operating on the spine,' said Martin. Lying on the trolley before he went into the theatre he was feeling pretty nervous, but a chance conversation with a hospital worker revealed a remarkable coincidence that was to put him at his ease. 'A porter came up to ask how I was and when I told him I was worried, he said, "Just take a look at this,"' said Martin. 'He lifted up his shirt and showed me a scar on his back. He had had the very same operation by the same surgeon that I was facing and he told me he had just run the London Marathon! He really put me at ease and that was the last thought on my mind before I went to sleep.'

As has been said earlier, Martin is a firm believer in using alternative as well as conventional medicine. 'I most certainly do not belong to that passionate band of people who say that orthodox medicine is rubbish,' he said. 'But it is a shame that alternative medicine is not fully accepted by the medical establishment. I have been using homeopathic remedies among other things for most of my adult life and I have learned quite a lot about them. Before my operation I had a myelogram, which involves a needle being inserted inside your spinal cavity to inject fluid so they can X-ray your spine. The procedure can be very painful as a result of spinal fluid leaking out of the puncture wound and I was told by the doctors to expect raging headaches within 10 minutes. The nurses told me they would give me strong painkillers as soon as I needed them but I thought I would prepare for it by using something of my own.'

Martin decided to get himself ready for the operation with homeopathic remedies and he amazed the doctors with the speed of his recovery. He used the Bach Rescue Remedy flower essences 6 times a day for 2 weeks. 'Then, when they put that 12-inch needle in my spine, I visualised a white light round the wound and I instructed the spinal fluid to stay where it was,' he said. 'Amazingly, when I got back to the ward I had no headache.'

The medical staff were clearly surprised. 'At first they wouldn't tell me what was going on but I heard two of them whispering about the fact that none of the fluid was escaping,' he said. 'The nurse kept coming over to see me afterwards and no one could believe I did not need any painkillers. When I explained I had used homeopathy and visualisation they just laughed.'

JUDGE JOHN DEED

'He is the kind of judge everyone would like to appear in front of,
if you were ever to go up the steps to the dock'
G F Newman on his creation John Deed

Award-winning author Gordon Frank Newman has always been controversial. Even the title of his uncompromisingly realistic first crime novel horrified some of Britain's more sensitive bookshop owners, but the unforgettable *Sir, You Bastard* sold some 200,000 copies even though some sniffy establishments politely refused to have it on public display. On television, his ground-breaking BBC police series *Law and Order* lifted the lid on the scandalous inadequacies of the justice system in the late 1970s and caused questions to be asked in the House of Commons. The 4 plays which made up the scintillating series were such a brilliantly crafted illustration of how corruption thrived among people who were supposed to be upholding the law that the Prison

Officers' Association brought in a ban on filming inside jails and the police were similarly outraged. It also drew a mesmeric central performance from actor Derek Martin (today better known as Charlie Slater in *EastEnders)* as devious Detective Inspector Fred Pyle. 'The scripts were just brilliant,' says Derek. 'They blew me away right from the start. They were brave, shocking and brutally honest. They had realism, humour and incredible energy. We all knew at the time that this guy was a very special writer. If only all television reached that standard.'

G F Newman also wrote the memorable Channel 4 series *The Nation's Health,* which exposed some of the appalling injustices of our hospitals and provoked a storm of protest from doctors. So when he came to write a series about a maverick judge with an awkward enthusiasm for the truth, every potential leading man in TV land was interested. But Newman only wanted one man for the job, his friend Martin Shaw. The two men share many principles, including vegetarianism. Both favour fairly radical politics and both have a compulsion to tell the truth, however uncomfortable. Newman created the role of the fiercely independent and highly sexed high court judge with Martin in mind because he wanted Deed to be attractive to women of all ages. Deed was to be a very out-of-the-ordinary high court judge, an idealist who was clearly seen as a renegade by most of his much more traditional colleagues. He had made it to the top of his profession very much on his own terms and was to have a rakish charm, a keen wit and a passionate belief in justice. Fearless and independent, he was loyal to state and sovereign rather than to the grubby civil servants and politicians who try to keep him under control. Very fortunately for the BBC and its viewers, Martin realised straight away that this was a rare opportunity to do inspirational drama on television and swiftly reached for his wig.

'I never miss the chance to work with G F Newman because he is one of TV's best writers,' said Martin. 'His writing is thought-provoking which is why I would have been enormously disappointed if *Judge John Deed* were dismissed as just a piece of entertainment. Of course it is meant to entertain, but you've got to exercise people's minds as well.'

The popularity of the show was pretty much instant and the BBC were delighted. The Corporation's head of continuing series, Mal Young, put it down simply to: 'Quality writing and a quality cast. What more could we ask for from a talent such as G F Newman, who is no stranger to dealing with taboo issues in a hard-hitting fashion.' And BBC head of drama Jane Tranter agreed. She sent out a statement to say: 'The first series of *Judge John Deed* proved extremely popular with audiences when it was shown and provoked a considerable reaction from the public, the legal profession and the critics.' Asked to explain what made the character of Judge John Deed so appealing, G F Newman thought for a moment and then answered: 'He is the kind of judge everyone would like to appear in front of, if you were ever to go up the steps to the dock. He appeals to most people because he pursues justice regardless of personal risk and a sense of justice is one of the highest human aspirations. Deed speaks out against all the petty rules and bureaucracy that frustrate us all, but that most of us don't speak out against.'

Martin Shaw agreed heartily with every word. He was

delighted to 'get Gordon Newman's work back onto mainstream television where it belongs'. Newman insisted that a knowledge of the law was not necessary to enjoy the programmes, even though they often involved highly complex legal cases. He said: 'No drama should stop or take time to explain the proceedings in a courtroom, but instead try to steer the reader through it in an intelligent way that leaves him or her with a clear understanding. What we get with this series is an intricate exploration of the Law, without patronising the audience. The Law is something which often frustrates and confuses people – especially in their own dealings with it. The Law is often arcane and impenetrable to us.'

Judge John Deed was quite the opposite. The combination of Newman's bold writing and Shaw's top-quality acting became a television triumph. It showed that small-screen drama can take on challenging subjects and educate as well as entertain. The rebellious streak running through his character certainly rang a bell with Martin. 'I love the way Judge John Deed is part of the Establishment, and yet he is always fighting against it,' he said. He certainly admires his character, particularly when he is at his most awkward. 'I do identify very much with Deed,' he said. 'Because the desire for justice is something the judge and I share. I identify strongly with his need to have the truth out, no matter what the cost. Also, it is nice to wield such extraordinary power.' Martin noted with relish that people stand up when a judge walks into the room and no one sits down until he is seated. The judge doesn't even carry a pencil from place to place – someone else does it for him! Wherever a high court judge sits he is 'the Sovereign' and always has to be accorded a similar level of respect.

As a television series *Judge John Deed* was remarkably well constructed, with its fascinating set-piece courtroom confrontations cleverly complemented by a well-selected cast. Jenny Seagrove is excellent as the dedicated Jo Mills but she is beautifully supported by Caroline Langrishe as Deed's troublesome ex-wife George and Sir Donald Sinden as his booming ex-father-in-law and old-school judge, Sir Joseph Channing. Young actress Louisa Clein fits in neatly as Deed's rebellious daughter Charlie, whose own career clashes so often with her father's. Newman's enthusiasm for women with men's names is by no means the only quirk of this highly individual series.

'I think viewers like the show because it treats them as intelligent beings,' said Martin. 'There is a depressing amount of poor television around nowadays and this is something different.' He clearly revels in the way the powers that be always want Deed to toe the line and do things their way while he is forever fiercely forging his own route. 'That's great,' he said. 'I have been led to believe that the legal profession love it.' Martin always likes to get right inside any part he plays and he confided that with Judge John Deed the pleasure was extra special. He said: It's rather marvellous to pretend that I am as clever as this person. If you learn the lines well enough and say them rapidly, it looks as though you know what you are talking about. Also, you get the vicarious pleasure of dishing out the sort of justice that I think most people want to see dished.' He believes there are several key similarities between being an actor and a barrister. 'Barristers have to dramatise,' he said. 'Barristers have to camp it up and choose when to be restrained and when to be loud. They have to be convincing and unfortunately both jobs require a very great deal of homework.'

Of course, most lawyers (not to mention the rest of the viewers) enjoy seeing the colourful and courageous legal eagle hurling himself into a highly energetic sex life with a string of extremely attractive partners. The 'briefs' Judge John Deed investigates are very varied and interesting. His on-off relationship with dedicated barrister lover Jo Mills, played by Jenny Seagrove, is one of the strengths that underpin the success of the series. 'Deed is much cleverer than me but I don't like his morality very much,' Martin said. 'He keeps sleeping around and wondering why Jo gets upset with it.'

He was not always happy with the womanising side of the character's nature. 'His addiction to having sex with as many women as possible shows a great flaw in his character,' said Martin. 'I admire him as a judge but I don't admire him as a person. The way the series is set up, Deed is a hero. He's Spider Man and he rights wrongs, but at the same time I think he wrongs women by hurting them – he hurts Jo Mills all the time. I said to Gordon Newman that if we're going to keep on doing this then we need some explanation of why Deed behaves like this – that's why Deed had therapy.'

The judge visited a therapist and managed to figure out that his commitment phobia stemmed from the death of his mother, who killed herself when he was just 10 years old. Ever since that rejection, divorcee Deed had never been able to properly commit to another woman.

In spite of how badly John Deed treats her, actress Jenny Seagrove insists that Martin himself is 'joyous' to work with. She explained that they have a shorthand between them and that they both work the same way. 'We both come from the school where detail is everything but it should never look as if you are acting,' said Jenny. 'If I'm doing something that he doesn't think is right, he'll whisper in my ear, "Jen, try something different," and I'll do the same for him. But there is no ego involved. It's not like we're giving each other notes – it's more that we're mates and we want the best for each other.' And in case that sounded as though working with Martin Shaw was rather more serious than it evidently is she was quick to point out that working on *Judge John Deed* was 'a lot of fun'. 'He's a very funny man,' said Jenny. 'And we play football together on the set in a quadrangle in Bushey – he's got a good right foot. He's a dab hand with a football in his robes.' The success of the series has surprised many of the cast and production team. Jenny Seagrove confessed she never imagined it would run for so long. 'Whoever thought it would be such a big hit?' she commented. 'I love the fact that I can take my dog to work and I love working with Martin and Gordon – it's a real pleasure.' She recognises that Jo Mills' tender yet traumatic relationship with John Deed is one of the reasons for the popularity of the show. 'People come up to me and ask me if I am going to marry him,' she said. 'Or they give me advice on how to deal with him, and that includes top lawyers.'

But with Gordon Newman's firm hand of control on the series, as producer as well as writer, the good judge always seems to stay based in reality. Just to be on the safe side the scripts are all checked over by lawyers before filming a single scene. 'I know a lot of them say, "Oh no, we wouldn't do it like that,"' said Martin, 'but lawyers have as many opinions as doctors and when you hear them rustling their papers and making mild clucking noises, you know you've got it right.'

After four highly enjoyable series, Martin Shaw turned 60 and wondered if he would be able to carry on the screen seductions much longer. Deed had already bedded his boss's wife and even his therapist in previous series, as well as the lovely Jo, but it seemed in Series Five that he was in danger of leaping into a bed too far as he prepared to sleep with a shapely claimant whose case he was hearing. It was seen to be such a flagrant breach of the rules that for a time Deed was banished from the bench by his fellow judges. 'Realistically speaking,' said Martin, 'I am not going to be able to carry on playing romantic roles much longer so it would be better, like [England cricket captain] Nasser Hussain, to quit while you're still able to score centuries instead of having people going, "Um, I don't think so." You don't want producers going, "We'll give him the bedroom scene but he'll need a ladder to get in and out of bed!"' He flatly refuses to take the sex-symbol tag seriously. 'It's hardly my favourite topic of conversation,' he said dryly. 'I don't particularly enjoy talking about it, I don't see the sex appeal thing at all. I read about it and sometimes I hear people say it and I think, "What are they on about? Are they winding me up?"'

Martin is always quick to give full credit to Gordon Newman for the enduring success of the series and points out that there are very few writers who can produce 6 episodes consecutively and maintain such a high standard. The star's favourite Deed story was the memorable encounter with the gentlemen and ladies of Her Majesty's Press. Martin is no fan of the less responsible journalists, so he was delighted when Deed locked up a group of reporters for contempt of court and criticised the media for deliberately pandering to the lowest common denominator in the public. 'These are two issues which are close to my heart so I tackled them with some relish,' he said with a smile. He also enjoyed it a great deal when his oldest son Luke guest-starred in one episode as Paul Sorrell, one of Jo Mills' junior barristers. In some of his scenes with Louise Clein, who plays his screen daughter Charlie, he also finds echoes of his relationship with his own daughter Sophie. 'I use my own experiences as a dad with Charlie,' he said. 'It's a very fortunate coincidence that Louisa really is like my daughter, both in looks and in nature, so it's easy to slip into the father–daughter relationship.'

There was no slacking in standards even by the time the sixth series arrived in 2006. Gordon Newman and Martin Shaw both insisted there must be no dumbing down. They were equally determined to make the courtroom drama remain as hard-hitting as ever. 'We're still controversial,' said Martin. 'The first episode includes a storyline concerning racism in the police service, along with a bit of cannibalism!'

The viewers voted with their remote controls and ratings stayed healthy for a series which began with a young black prisoner being brutally murdered a week before his release by a known racist in their shared prison cell. The Prison Service quickly starts to circle the wagons and blames overcrowding for the rising tensions but Deed's questioning reveals that in fact the jail was not full at the time. It becomes clear that the killing was a much more sinister crime than anyone could have first imagined. Deed's success in court was cleverly interwoven with new difficulties with the lovely Jo. She becomes distant and when he confronts her, she tells him she is learning to live without him. For a tantalising time she hides the fact that her old flame Marc has returned from South Africa wanting to marry her. Of course Deed discovers what's going on, but the friction is always restrained and beautifully delivered. 'I love filming the show,' said Martin. 'After five years, the cast are old friends so it is very comfortable on set.'

DALGLIESH

*'I'm very excited by the idea of seeing Martin up on the screen.
He's an intelligent and thoughtful actor. Physically, he's a very
attractive character – and one likes one's characters to be attractive'*
P D James on Martin taking over as Adam Dalgliesh

The brilliant poetry-writing detective Adam Dalgliesh has a very special place in the heart of acclaimed multi award-winning crime writer P D James. With tender loving care she created her hero as a good professional policeman who was also a sensitive human being. 'I gave him qualities that I admired personally,' she said, 'because I thought if I don't like him personally I am going to get extremely bored with him, if I'm lucky enough to be able to carry through a series. Also, I didn't want to worry about his love life so I rather callously killed off his wife and child.'

Over the last 44 years, the captivating investigations of the quiet and introspective policeman have became a worldwide success story. Ever since he first appeared in James's 1962 novel *Cover Her Face,* sales of Dalgliesh adventures have never flagged. And the writer's affection for her creation has grown and grown. In the books he is tall, dark and handsome with a distinct hint of Mr Darcy from *Pride and Prejudice*; on television he was Roy Marsden. ITV made 10 films of James's books which drew large audiences. The beautifully crafted novels were adapted with varying degrees of success but in the mind of the writer they were never quite perfect. Roy Marsden is a fine actor, but he does not exactly ooze sexual charisma. He made a decent effort of becoming Adam Dalgliesh without ever quite fulfilling the dreams deep in the imagination of P D James, so when the BBC decided to try its hand at the Dalgliesh stories it was time for a change.

P D James wanted a star who could light up the screen in the same as way her words illuminated the page, and she had drawn Adam Dalgliesh as the son of a Norfolk country rector who had inherited a share in a converted windmill on the county's coast. Somehow, that fitted in with the choice of Martin Shaw to breathe new life into the cerebral sleuth, so James was delighted. At last she had a star who could convey with his dashing good looks and undeniable screen presence what she had been seeing in her mind's eye for half her lifetime.

Before he began rehearsals Martin went to meet James and he was full of trepidation because he desperately wanted her approval. 'She's very formidable and extraordinarily powerful, but inspiring,' he said. 'She's a Dame and she's been on the bestseller list for 40 years. I realised I had to be vetted by her, but she knew all my work and was absolutely divine. She was a bit concerned as I wanted to wear spectacles as Dalgliesh. Normally I wear contact lenses but I wanted to look as different as possible from Judge John Deed. Dalgliesh is very perceptive and sharp-eyed, and she was afraid that the glasses might distract from that. I think what sold me to her was I said, "But he sees with his heart, doesn't he, not with his eyes?" which is true and she went "Aaah," in her lovely grand way.'

Martin was an inspired choice, and P D James was clearly thrilled when he agreed to take over the role. 'I'm very excited by the idea of seeing Martin up on the screen,' she said. 'He is an intelligent and thoughtful actor, so he's able to do what I think is so difficult, which is to convey to the viewer what is going on between his ears. Physically, he is a very attractive character – and one likes one's characters to be attractive.'

It's difficult to imagine a more ringing endorsement, and Jane Tranter, BBC controller of drama commissioning, was equally enthusiastic about Martin taking over Dalgliesh's mantle. 'Commander Adam Dalgliesh has become something of a national hero, and Martin Shaw brings an immediate freshness and emotional intensity to the role,' she said.

As ever, Martin had chosen a role that was more difficult than it first appeared. It was his first role as a detective, discounting the chief constable he played in *The Chief*, and he summed up his new character thus: 'Dalgliesh is very bright and he thinks a lot; he's a poet and artistic. He's one of the hardest characters I've ever had to play because in the novels he's an observer. He is the eyepiece through which the audience sees everything. This is quite hard to translate into a character on screen.'

Martin spent some fascinating time in the company of P D James herself, but he says that he didn't ask her much, nor did she volunteer very much about how she thought he should play Dalgliesh. She was happy to leave it up to Martin, who pointed out: 'I know it sounds blasphemous, but there really isn't a strong character there. The good thing about that is, that within certain boundaries he could be played many different ways. He is somebody who is very still and if you are really thinking what the character should be thinking, the audience can pick it up.'

But there were plenty of clues in the writing: according to P D James, when Adam Dalgliesh was a very young detective and new to the CID, an experienced officer took him to one side and told him that all the motives for murder begin with the letter L – love, lust, lure and loathing. He added: 'They'll tell you, laddie, that the most dangerous emotion is hatred. Don't believe them. The most dangerous emotion is love.' Martin grasped the writer's perceptions with both hands as he took charge and Adam Dalgliesh took on a new lease of life.

The Dalgliesh comeback began with the two-parter *Death In Holy Orders* and presented the intellectual commander with probably the most difficult and personal case of his career. Returning to St. Anselm's, the theological college where he spent many happy days in his youth, he finds this isolated windswept outpost on the Suffolk cliffs is the setting for frenzied murders by a serial killer. Viewers welcomed Dalgliesh's return, and so did the critics. 'The BBC poured good acting like golden syrup over *Death In Holy Orders* and served it up in two generous helpings,' said the *Guardian*. And the *Daily Mail* said: 'A wonderful gallery of veteran British actors... Shaw has brought the detective right up to date...'

Jane Tranter was thrilled by the general reaction: 'The success of *Death In Holy Orders* confirmed the public's appetite for intelligent and thoughtful crime dramas, and the enduring popularity of P D James,' she enthused, and quickly commissioned another two-parter, *The Murder Room,* that screened early in 2005 with Dalgliesh tackling murder and adultery while following a trail that led him right up to the House of Lords.

Margaret Enefer, the producer of *Death In Holy Orders*, saw the intricate plot as perfect material for gripping drama aimed at those with a penchant for demanding detective thrillers. Martin's portrayal of the poetic detective was a powerful reminder, she said, of his talent and position as one of the country's most versatile actors.

Martin himself was delighted to have pulled it off. 'It's wonderfully well written, totally different from *Judge John Deed*, and best of all it is filmed in Norfolk,' he said. 'Sometimes I really do feel fortunate.'

MARTIN SHAW – A MAN FOR ALL SEASONS

'Watching your dad getting his head chopped off every night
does take it out of you – although it's probably worse for him!'
Martin's daughter Sophie Shaw on sharing the
stage with her father in *A Man For All Seasons*

M artin Shaw was a 15-year-old schoolboy who was just starting to show an interest in Shakespeare when *A Man For All Seasons*, which has been described as the greatest history play of the modern era, was first performed in London on 1 July 1960. And he was a 21-year-old student at the London Academy of Music and Dramatic Art in 1966 when Robert Bolt's play was turned into a film that earned an Oscar for its star, Paul Scofield – then 1 of only 5 Britons to have received the Best Actor award in 40 years.

Bolt's play was a timeless personal story based on the sixteenth-century politico-religious conflict between the adulterous King Henry VIII and the Catholic Chancellor of

England, Sir Thomas More. Henry wanted to divorce his ageing first wife, Catherine of Aragon, who had failed to provide him with the heir he wanted so that he could marry his mistress Anne Boleyn. Because the Catholic faith did not permit divorce, Henry decided to break with the church and form the Church of England, allowing him to marry whomsoever he pleased. The highly principled More, however, would not publicly endorse Henry's break from Rome. For More, a lawyer, writer, scholar and churchman there is no choice and it ultimately costs him his head.

Bolt's basic dramatic theme was of the conscience of a minister of the crown being challenged by the king's imperious point of view, which maintains that the lack of explicit support to an erring king is tantamount to disloyalty. He seized on this very human dilemma that occurs whenever expediency confronts integrity, wrote a fascinating and powerful play and created one of modern drama's greatest tragic heroes.

A Man For All Seasons was rapturously received as a stage play back in the 1960s and earned Scofield sensational notices for his performance as Sir Thomas More. And the film, which followed 6 years later, for which Bolt also wrote the screenplay, scooped a further 5 Oscars to add to Scofield's own, and 7 British Academy Awards into the bargain. The movie, and Scofield's brilliant performance, made a deep impression on all who saw it – not least a young drama student like Martin. But, never in his wildest dreams can he have imagined that, some 40 years later, he would take on the stage role of Sir Thomas More and give a performance that some would say bears favourable comparison with Scofield's.

Martin, by all accounts, had wanted to play More for a long time and he was given the chance in the autumn of 2005 by producer Kenwright with whom he has enjoyed a long and highly successful association. He starred in Bill Kenwright's first-ever big West End hit, *The Country Girl,* back in 1983 and the two men have been close friends ever since. Like Martin, as a young actor, Kenwright, too, had a stint in *Coronation Street* and he has frequently expressed his admiration for Martin as a supremely talented and courageous actor. 'They used to say that the best four words in the English language are, "Harrison Ford says yes," and for me the best four words were, "Martin Shaw says yes,"' the producer has said of the actor. 'We absolutely hit it off. When I was an actor myself, the one I always wanted to be was Martin Shaw – I just thought he had everything.'

Kenwright is a perceptive and knowledgeable observer of the dramatic scene who realises the everyday injustice of actors not always getting the credit that their performances deserve, especially if they happen to be working in television. He said: 'It really upsets me that actors like Martin, and my partner Jenny Seagrove (who plays Jo Mills in *Judge John Deed*), who are considered "television actors", don't get the kind of recognition they deserve. He's such a brave actor.' When Kenwright acquired the rights to *A Man For All Seasons*, Martin was busy with television commitments but he was prepared to wait for two years until his leading actor was available.

Typically, it was another brave step for Martin to take it on, given that the role was so synonymous with Scofield's much-lauded stage and screen performances, a portrayal Martin has described as 'iconic'. Martin explained his feelings about the role to *The Lady* magazine: 'It was a problem for me mentally at first. It [*A Man For All Seasons*] is my favourite film and he [Paul Scofield] is my favourite actor. He is one of the three finest actors we have ever produced – the others being Anthony Hopkins and [Laurence] Olivier, whom I worked with at the National Theatre. Scofield has a genius for understatement and honesty, the two things most difficult for an actor, because you really have to make an impact and you have to move people.' Certainly it was a daunting challenge, but it was one challenge that Martin simply knew he had to accept. 'It's the sort of opportunity an actor dreams about,' he said. 'So even though it was not easy I don't think I could have lived with myself if I hadn't taken it on.'

Long before the production reached the West End on its 10-theatre tour of the country, Martin was receiving rave notices in the provinces and there were favourable mentions, too, for his daughter Sophie, who had won the role of More's daughter Margaret, or Meg. In the past, one or two opportunities had arisen for Sophie to act in the same production as her father but she had fought shy of them, preferring instead to make her own way. But the chance of appearing alongside her dad in such a prestigious play as *A Man For All Seasons* was too good to miss.

In press interviews, she was keen to stress that she auditioned for the part of Margaret and when she was chosen to play Meg, she received a letter from the director Michael Rudman shortly afterwards stressing that she had won the part entirely on her own merit and that he wanted her to be aware of that. 'That meant an awful lot to me,' she said. She also confirmed that Martin had hankered after playing More for years and that he had always said it would be great if Sophie could play his daughter.

Sophie, 31, described the relationship between More and Meg as wonderful, full of warmth and humour, a father and daughter who saw themselves as friends and intellectual sparring partners. 'We have a not-too-dissimilar relationship,' she said of her own relationship with Martin. 'We're very close and loving. We're also intellectual sparring partners but we're combative in a warm way. So a lot of the relationship between Thomas and Meg, you get for free.'

The addition of Sophie to the cast meant that Martin had completed a remarkable family hat trick acting alongside each of his offspring, all of whom, like him, had trained at LAMDA. Sons Joe and Luke had appeared with him in *Rhodes* and *Judge John Deed* respectively, and now he was proud to have Sophie treading the boards with him. Sophie said she saw the benefits from day one: the first day at rehearsals was usually terrifying wondering if you'd know anybody and whether they'd like you, but with her dad there, at least there was one person she'd know, someone she could slope off to lunch with and someone who was legally obliged to like her! 'Watching your dad getting his head chopped off every night does take it out of you – although it's probably worse for him!' she said.

A Man For All Seasons opened in London's West End to wonderful notices with the critics unanimous in their praise for Martin. Writing in *The Times*, Benedict Nightingale said that before he saw director Michael Rudman's revival of the play, he reckoned he could count on the thumb of one hand the actor who could successfully play its central character. Surely, he said, only Paul Scofield had the gravity and charisma to play Sir Thomas More, and he was the wrong age by about 30 years, and more or less retired. 'But Martin Shaw makes me realise that I need two hands and two thumbs,' he wrote. 'He's often overlooked when we are listing leading actors, but he has a quality that tends to elude even Ian McKellen and Derek Jacobi. This is stillness and, to get metaphoric and possibly pretentious, the stillness of a pool whose bottom we can't see.'

Cathy Pryor, in *The Independent*, was no less complimentary. She described Martin as '… a fine actor with strong stage presence.' She added: 'I'll admit I found myself thinking: "Could he ever be as good as Paul Scofield?"' These reservations, though, had largely been dispelled by the end of the second and final act, by which time the play had come into its own. 'Shaw makes a splendidly scruffy and believable Sir Thomas, with exactly the right mix of integrity, wit and gravitas. He wins our sympathy throughout – not an easy job…'

Simon Edge in the *Daily Express* said: 'Forty-five years after its first performance, the play is back in the West End with Martin Shaw in magnificent form as Sir Thomas.' He went on to say: 'Shaw, sporting a blond Michael Heseltine mane which turns grey as he languishes in a cell, puts in a towering performance. His Thomas is a man of gentle wit and quiet dignity but we also see the self-righteous zealot not far below the surface.' In the *Daily Mail* Patrick Marmion enthused: 'Affable, bluff, intransigent and proud to begin with, Shaw adds melancholy, rage, terror and, eventually, dignity to a well-seasoned performance. By the end he is limp with emotional exhaustion, but still manages proudly to lift the hair from his neck on behalf of his cowled executioner.'

Just as Martin had managed temporarily to erase the memory of Marlon Brando many years before when playing Stanley Kowalski in *A Streetcar Named Desire*, so now he had produced a performance to rival Paul Scofield's in *A Man For All Seasons*.

Martin Shaw as Sir Thomas More was clearly meant to be. Many months before he had received a Paul Scofield Award for his acting at a London ceremony. The inscription from Scofield himself that came with the award read: 'To Martin Shaw, an actor for all seasons.' It was prophetic indeed. 'Scofield didn't even know he wanted to play the part,' said Bill Kenwright. 'So it's serendipity that we're doing it.'

EPILOGUE

'I would either be dead or in a mental home by now if
I hadn't changed my lifestyle'
Martin Shaw

The steely blue eyes are the first thing many people notice on meeting Martin Shaw. Steady and unwavering, they seem to bore right into you. He might well need contact lenses but he still appears to be gazing deep inside you in search of any surprises. Some actors avoid eye contact and indeed one or two even have it in their contracts that it is never under any circumstances to be engaged in by underlings of any description, but Shaw revels in being 100 per cent direct. He intensely dislikes misunderstandings and generally regards being interviewed as about as appealing as a sinus wash.

This is perhaps not completely surprising, as journalists have given him a pretty rough time over the years. If he had £1 for every time he has been described as 'TV tough guy' then he

247

would be able to buy his own vintage air force, which would doubtless please him greatly. He has explained his passionate views on vegetarianism, recalled his upbringing in Birmingham, and opened up on his unusual philosophy of life many times to promote the latest play or film or television series. At times dealing with the gentlemen and ladies of the Press can be wearing, but the authors were present when one particularly pompous Scottish television writer employed by the *Daily Express* buttonholed Martin and asked him if he was going to return to the role of Eddie Shoestring. Now that other fine Midlands actor Trevor Eve might hail from Sutton Coldfield, just down the road from Martin's roots, but they are two very different people. To his eternal credit Martin saw the funny side.

Not that he is always so easy-going. One of the authors was doing an interview with Martin in the elegant setting of the Sprowston Manor Hotel in Norwich when a middle-aged lady nervously approached and politely asked for an autograph. Martin told her curtly that he was busy, and quickly sent her packing with her eyes filling with tears of disillusioned astonishment. 'I get that all the time, it's so annoying,' he said. 'Now where was I?' It would almost have been quicker to sign the name and keep a fan happy, but to Martin it was an unfair and unwanted imposition, and he waved away a half-hearted opinion to the contrary. 'All you owe the public is a good performance,' he said. It was a flash of irritation that seemed out of character. The remark you most often hear when talking to people who have met Martin Shaw is along the lines of: 'I thought he would be a pain in the neck, but he was absolutely charming and very, very professional.'

Shaw has a glittering career spanning almost 40 years. Almost never out of fashion and hardly ever unwillingly out of work, he has chosen difficult, challenging roles and always spurned the easy option. Other actors love to work with him because he is very good and exceptionally generous.

The big change in his life came when he was a young man who was drinking too much and in some danger of squandering his remarkable God-given talent. He remains grateful to his drama school friend Luke Hardy for steering him away from alcohol and towards vegetarianism. His night of revelation began, he recalls, as 'the usual vegetarian-carnivore joust'. But it went on until three o'clock in the morning and Martin found himself defeated. It was part of his character to accept the truth of the argument. The choice was made for him there and then, though at first he was not completely happy. 'I thought it was going to be too difficult,' said Martin. 'There were only two vegetarian restaurants in London then – Cranks and The Nut House. You can work out for yourself what the prevailing attitudes were. Now you can find vegetarian restaurants wherever you go. Times have changed, and for the better so far as I am concerned.'

A strict vegetarian and teetotaller, ever since his night of truth with Luke he has been a devout follower of the spiritual leader Charan Singh. 'It has saved my life,' he says. 'I would either be dead or in a mental home by now if I hadn't changed my lifestyle.' The healthy lifestyle has fashioned a successful life. Martin insists he has to be in peak physical form to cope with the pressures that come with the job. 'I have known successful, apparently healthy actors who have abused their bodies and been drunk for 25 years, but I could not operate that way.'

Most of the time he takes great care to make sure that he eats very sensibly. Yet even he is not perfect and sometimes he treats himself to food he likes that he knows full well is not good for him, such as fried food, cream doughnuts and chips, but his body soon rebels against too much forbidden food. 'I just monitor what's happening,' says Martin. 'The greatest benefit of my personal fitness is that I know what's happening. I am not a fitness fanatic or anything but I know I am very fit for my age and I think it's because after years of being vegetarian I am very sensitive to what's happening with my body so I know what to do. If I am feeling all sort of swollen, I know how to stop that and if my energy level goes down I know how to raise it again so I can keep myself working at my best. If I want to be really strict, if I've got an incredibly tough part coming up, a stage role that I need to be superfit for, then I know what to do. I know quite a lot about alternative medicine and stuff. I don't work out, it's just the diet. I've got some work-out stuff which is there if I need it. I've got a bicycle that I use whenever I'm in London – apart from the fact it is ecologically sound, I like to do my bit. It doesn't make any sense to drive in London, it's too expensive, you can't park when you get there and it's much quicker by bike.

'It was a moral decision to become a vegetarian and it remains a moral decision, but the health benefits are a very fortunate side issue. You get signals from your body. We all do if we are tuned in properly to our bodies. I feel my muscles aching, tiredness and my eyesight starts going.' Then it is time for a severe cleansing routine, eating raw vegetables, drinking liquorice-based herb tea and a potion he makes up in a blender from oil, garlic, lemon juice and orange juice to cleanse the liver. Without eight hours sleep a night he knows he cannot shift into top gear and ideally he likes an afternoon nap when he can fit one in.

Shaw and *Judge John Deed* writer Gordon Newman are fellow vegans and frequently stand together on vegetarian issues. Martin said: 'If people were taken, before they eat their meals, to a factory farm and saw the degradation and torture they are party to, I don't believe that many of them would want to go ahead and eat their meal.' Martin joined with stars, including Sir Paul McCartney and Joanna Lumley to make a video produced by the pressure group Viva, which campaigns against factory farming. Viva say 45 billion animals were slaughtered in the world in 2003, and 1 billion of them in Britain, and most were factory farmed. Martin feels a sincere and deep anger over what he sees as this fundamental injustice.

But many of his public pronouncements have the effect of making Martin appear, as he himself fears: 'a pompous prat'. He is not a prat and he is not pompous. An actor who asked not to be named told the authors that he was struggling very badly financially until Martin found out and quietly helped him out, on the strict understanding that it would remain between them. 'I'm not giving you any details,' said our source. 'But just take it from me, Martin Shaw is a bloody good bloke. He is as straight as a die and he came close to saving my life. I know that I am by no means the only person he has helped. If there were more people like Martin Shaw around, this country would be a better place.' Martin certainly has a soft-hearted side. He insists that the first thing he would grab in a fire are his cats. He loves them with a passion that he knows perfectly well is irrational, but he loves them just the same.

Of course, he might well have been a major Hollywood star if events had happened only slightly differently, but dreaming about what might have been does not keep him awake at night. 'Part of the philosophy I have been following is not to have any regrets,' he said. 'A regret is a waste of time… I hope that doesn't make me sound like a pompous prat either.'

The living person he admires most in life is the veteran Labour politician Tony Benn. In most politicians Martin finds integrity sadly lacking but he regards Benn as an inspirational figure. But many aspects of modern life depress Shaw. He hates how values have deteriorated, the inevitable destruction of our environment and the rule of big business. Those themes might sound fashionable nowadays but even as quite a young man, Martin was regretting the passing of a gentler age.

Of course, having split with Vicky Kimm in late 2004 and now with three marriages behind him, Martin Shaw's private life is not exactly studded with happy endings but he remains on good terms with almost everyone who has passed through his life.

His idea of perfect happiness was once described as a 'cross-country flight in my biplane without getting lost.' And he said that his favourite smell is a hot vintage aircraft engine. But his beloved old 1940s Stearman bi-plane came to what looked like a sad finish when it crashed as it attempted to take off from a Norfolk airfield in August 2004. Martin Shaw was not on board as the plane had been leased by the Old Buckenham Airfield, but he was there and he saw the plane crash. It overturned and the pilot managed to pull his passenger out before a fire started. Both were treated at the scene for minor injuries by paramedics but Martin was deeply relieved that no one was hurt. The crash took place on a Sunday evening and next day he was again at the airfield to inspect the damage. The accident report recorded that the take-off run appeared normal, but once in the air the plane failed to climb properly and it had reached just 100 feet when the pilot decided to bring it down and attempted to make an emergency landing in a field. One possible cause was unusual 'thermal activity', which could have resulted in potentially dangerous temporary tailwinds. Martin was upset at the damage to the plane he had bought for £80,000 10 years earlier but he was of course much more relieved that no one was hurt.

The local paper, the *Eastern Daily Press*, reported the accident in some detail and drew unexpected praise from the actor, who is not known for his affection for journalists. He wrote to tell the newspaper: 'I am very quick to criticise the Press when they get it wrong, but your report was accurate and sympathetic, qualities rare in today's media climate. Vicky and I are saddened by the loss of this historic aircraft, but thank God no one was badly injured.' The American World War II plane was one of the strongest aircraft ever constructed and is famous for protecting its occupants in a crash. Martin pledged to attempt a repair job, stating: 'If we can find a way to restore any elements of the wreck into a complete Stearman, it will be done and its good-natured growl will be back in our skies.'

Getting away from it all is essential for Shaw. One of his favourite places is his remote Scottish croft. He loves to go up there, particularly with his children. He still enjoys boys' toys and told one of the authors with great enthusiasm: 'I've got a "tricycle" in my cottage – it's actually a four-wheel-drive all-terrain vehicle. I've got two of those. They go absolutely everywhere and we go up the half-mountain/half-hill behind the cottage and we can actually get to the summit. My son was the first one to get to the summit on the bike but in the process one of the bikes got dropped and cost me £600 to have it put right again. It was a challenge and he was determined he was going to be the first, and he was. But now we can all get to the top.

'The Scottish place is totally away from it all,' said Martin with relish. 'It is in a real wilderness.' He laughs at the idea that he is a great landowner and explains: 'The amount of land I own around me is completely irrelevant because the house has thousands of square miles of Scotland around it. And because it is not on a road or anything it really doesn't matter how big it is. I don't know how much acreage there is, it is very small. I live up there very simply and sometimes I go up there and spend long periods of time on my own and don't notice it. People ask me if I find it difficult being on my own and I've never thought about it – I don't notice, I watch TV. If I was up there and there was no TV, I wouldn't like that. I am not one of those people who sit there in front of the fire and contemplate the ceiling. I do like the ritual of getting in, making a meal, eating the meal and watching TV. Sometimes I go up there with my children but I don't mind being on my own. I am happy with my own company sometimes. It doesn't freak me out.'

Shaw doesn't worry about work but of course now he doesn't need to. He insists he never has been the anxious type. 'The only thing I worry about is that sort of creeping necessity to make a living,' says Martin. 'I remember years ago Peter Gill who was then director of the Royal Court, saying, "Don't get married and keep your needs very compact, otherwise you limit your choices as an actor." And of course it's true. As your lifestyle gradually expands, you begin to realise that to live at the very basic simple level you need to earn more and more money. And that's the only demerit of being on a fairly comparatively elevated level for such a long time because when you are out of work, which happens a lot, you have suddenly got all these things to keep going and paying for. And that's why I work so hard, I guess.'

Martin's proudest achievement is his children, who have all followed his career path. 'I have got three of the most wonderful children anybody has ever had,' he says. 'Once they had made their decisions to go into acting I have encouraged them. I've told them that it was precarious when I started, but by the time they were starting there are something like double the number of applicants for less than half the chances. The situation is pretty bad. I have got friends who are very good actors who don't work very much. I have got no illusions about it – it's luck, Absolutely plain and simple luck. You have to be able to do it, but every competent actor can do it. There are another hundred who have equal qualifications but just haven't been so lucky. I think attitude is a lot to do with it as well. I have no difficulty in hanging onto that strange oriental paradox which is very difficult for the western mind, which is that the less anxious you are about getting on the more it will happen.'

He admits that his positive attitude to life only came gradually. 'It was something I had to learn,' he said, 'and that's part of luck you know because I think all of life is about finding one's teachers – not necessarily schoolteachers. But it's first of all identifying the problem and then going to a teacher who will solve that problem for you. So I just kept finding myself pointing in the right direction to overcome the next personal crisis or the next personal challenge. I don't want to stop – to me it's all a climb. I don't think it's an exhausting one. It's a climb I hope I have got some control over in that I can tie the rope occasionally and hang back and have a fag, but it's definitely onwards and upwards always.'

'I worry for my kids but I think that in the choice of career, parental responsibility only goes so far and I don't think it would have been right for me to say no, nor would it make any difference. I think my responsibility extends as far as making sure they know what the difficulties are, but it would be really unfair for me to do anything other than encourage them because all they have seen is success and all I can say is that it's not all like this – it's good luck. It's good fortune.'

For such a private person, he is very open about some aspects of his life. He told one of the authors how he benefits from taking time out at retreats. 'I do have a part of me that is quite monastic,' he said, 'And not in a self-flagellatory way. It is just that most people have found that sensory deprivation opens up other doors. I have done several retreats at Buddhist places where you don't speak and take the vow of silence, and you don't make eye contact with people and you walk round mindfully and very slowly sometimes. And the extraordinary thing is that how unselfish it is. It really amazed me because when you sit down and have a meal, and you are surrounded by people who equally can't speak or make eye contact, you are terribly aware of what other people might want. They can't say, "Pass the salt," or "Can you give me the bread," or "I haven't got a knife." So you need to be aware not only of yourself but of other people in case somebody else needs something. And there was an extraordinary and quite minor insight into how unselfish these retreats are and I didn't find it too hard. The almost suspension of thought is just the delight of being.

'If you are surrounded by distractions (which are wonderful – I like them as well, particularly things like aeroplanes and cars) ... it doesn't give you any chance. It's all extraction from being, and finally whatever it is – everything, people, objects – everything is transitory and everything you are ever left with is your own being and if you never give yourself the chance to appreciate what you are missing, what life is really about. So periodically these moments of solitude and introspection give you time to experience what and who you are. And it actually is fantastic but you have to go through all those prejudicial barriers that are fed into you like "Oh, it's egotistical" or "It is selfish and you must never love yourself." Once you have broken all those barriers down, it's extraordinary, the joyfulness of being. I do it for about a week. For me frankly that is not a long time and I always feel reluctant to start speaking again. When they say, "Right, the vow of silence is now broken and you may now speak," I've seen people actually freak out, literally fling themselves on the ground hysterical and screaming after two days because they can't stand it.

'We have no free will and everything is destined, but we must behave as though we create our own destiny so we have to be positive and bring good fortune to ourselves through our attitude, so the bottom line is, I believe, we can't influence anything at all. It does seem to be a rule of the universe that people are victims, attract victimisation and people who think I will never succeed don't somehow.'

In spite of his peace-loving philosophy, Martin is well aware that he possesses a temper. 'No one can help the way they are,' he said. 'I can only remember losing my temper three or four times in my life. I can be very petulant, but in a temper I go quiet, go white and speak very quietly.' He recalled the two worst incidents. The first was triggered by a disagreement over a taxi in London's Sloane Square after he had just opened at the Royal Court. He had a row with an American. 'I was with two girls and I opened the door when the cab arrived and he jumped the queue and jumped right in,' said Martin. 'I said, "Hey, you, piss off!" And I slowly pulled him out of the taxi. As I turned round to open the door he was waiting for me. He smashed me in the mouth. I was inside the cab going berserk. I was going for the cab door and my intention was to kill him. The taxi driver said, "You're f*****g crazy." I had really lost my temper.'

Martin can become very intense when discussing his

emotions. 'Anger can be very subtle,' he said. 'It expresses itself in petulance, swearing, all kinds of things.' He said he found release in expressing feeling: 'Even in sex you lose discrimination. You would be surprised how the truth makes life simpler. Even saying something to a woman like, "I find you very sexually attractive but I am not going to make a pass at you, because I am already with somebody else." Expressing that feeling can help express an emotion later on.

'The sort of reaction does depends on the girl. Some say, "Wow, thanks for telling me." And that is it. But other times it is all inside your own heads. "What happens if he offers to drive me home? Should I go with him?" On the other side it is: "If I offer to drive her home does it look like, you know?" Very often they are not with each other at all. When two mates meet they do not have to worry. So if there is something going on in my head I tell them. If it has produced a negative reaction I can put it right by saying, "How do you feel?" They might say, "I feel you should not say such things." I say, "No, that is not a feeling, that is an opinion." It is surprising how relaxed they are after that. They can say, "Oh, I feel upset. Or I feel good and I am glad that is out of the way."'

Martin prefers women who do not smoke, drink or eat meat, and he admits that this cuts the field down. He laughs. 'It does limit you but there are enough, though. Women have said to me, "I find you sexually attractive." And I say, "Thank you very much." But I get embarrassed too. But if I do, I say I am embarrassed.'

Relationships are not an area he feels happy discussing in public. After living in the public arena so much it is hardly surprising. 'I don't care about myself but I will not talk about other people's feelings,' he says. 'It is not fair.' He switches to safer ground, his love of the country.

Martin Shaw loves the countryside very deeply and he was quite prepared to join forces with more than 150 fellow villagers from Hingham, southwest of Norwich to speak up at a planning hearing to try to save a quiet valley that was said to be one of Norfolk's largest and most unspoilt wetlands. The protestors feared the area faced housing or agricultural development and asked for it to be awarded the same kind of protection as other land closer to Norwich. They told a government-appointed land inspector that they feared building might one day be permitted. The inspector agreed to view the area and Shaw was pleased. 'This seems to be a significant step forward,' he said.

Now in his sixties, he insists he would like to slow down, but that is much easier said than done. He claims to be wary of making detailed plans for the future. 'I try not to have them because any expectation, in my experience, is an excuse to be disappointed. My hope is that I don't fall into penury, don't suffer ill-health and that I am able to support myself and be satisfied. I don't have sufficient put by to say I don't need to work, but I have had a very lucky, very blessed career.'

INDEX